**CRESCENT BOOKS
NEW YORK**

Above Maria Schneider, complaisant among the suds in *Last Tango in Paris* (1972).
Right Starlet at the window – a still more youthful Maria Schneider, here mildly active as a voyeur on her movie début in Vadim's *Helle* (1970).

RICHARD WORTLEY
Erotic Movies

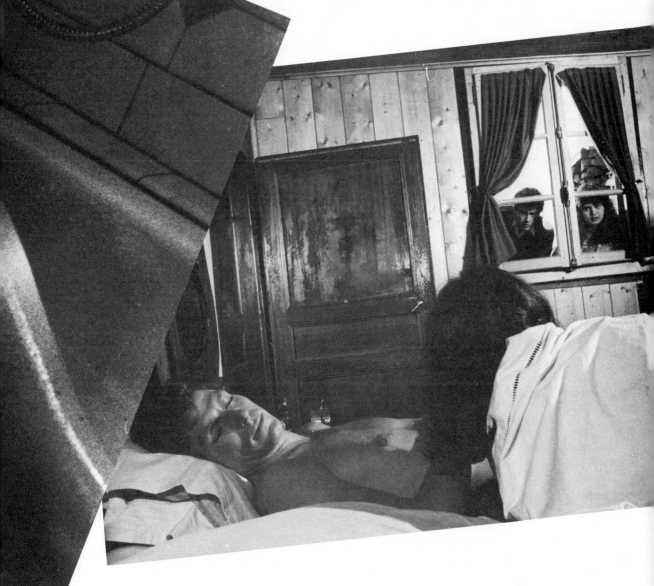

GENERAL EDITOR: SHERIDAN MORLEY

Copyright © Roxby Press Limited 1975

ISBN: 0-517-16826X

Library of Congress Catalog Card
Number 75-15167

First edition 1975
Reprinted 1977, 1979, 1980, 1981

This edition is published by Crescent Books,
distributed by Crown Publishers, Inc., by
arrangement with Roxby Press Limited

Made by Roxby Press Productions,
98 Clapham Common Northside,
London, SW4 9SG

Printed and bound in Spain by
Novograph, S. A., Madrid
Depósito Legal: M-17225-1981

ISBN: 0—517—16826X

INTRODUCTION

Erotic, from the Greek *erotikos* meaning sexual love, tends to suggest the stronger forms of physical togetherness. In this book I have set out to examine *sensuality* as much as physical action, not least because the former is more subtle and, in the main, less repetitive.

In discussing erotica in the movies, we are concerned with a medium ideally suited to represent the human form both in motion and repose – provided the bone structure, etc., is there in the first place and the lighting cameraman and wardrobe mistress are in suitable attendance to add the necessary finesse. In such a world, appearances and their presentation are naturally all-important. Thus it is common, for example, for movie stars to want only certain cameramen to film them, or a particular stills photographer to handle their publicity shots. Raquel Welch and 'her' photographer, Terry O'Neill, are a case in point.

Once the basics of outward appearance have been settled, what happens next to the actor or actress travelling the road to Eros is largely dictated by the plot and the director's interpretation of it. The director must also heed other guidelines: in simple terms, these usually stem from a national or regional censor, whose task is to see that appropriate respect is paid to the social *mores* of the time.

From an historical point of view, it would seem natural to expect the evolution of the movies to show some sort of linear progression from extreme censorship to total freedom. Up to a point, the cinema since its invention at the end of the last century has moved along such a line – reaching, to date, what one might call freedom with an X certificate. But within this span of some eighty years there have been surprises enough to disturb the smooth flow of history. At a very early date there were, for example, the exotic spectaculars of Cecil B. De Mille, and later on the still more surprising spectaculars of Busby Berkeley. Of course, the 'rules' of what any particular country will allow to be shown have varied not only with time but from one country to another. As an instance of this one can cite the progress of the French and Swedish film-makers: up to fifteen years ago they were noticeably ahead – not just in Europe but worldwide – in the box-office race for bodily exposure. Today that predominance is less marked.

These are some of the considerations that have influenced my approach to writing this book. It became clear that simply to chart a collection of relevant movies in date order would be a less rewarding *modus operandi* than to select certain underlying themes, which is what I have done. At the same time it was necessary to accept that in any such treatment overlaps would be bound to occur here and there; these, I hope, have been kept to a tolerable minimum. In setting down my ideas, I have also had to bear in mind that eroticism in general has never been acceptable to all. In the cinema one consequence has been to

Top Nudity plus 'It': Clara Bow, afloat in 1927.
Top right Patricia Medina, provocative in black, is nonetheless frightened by the Monster Who Knew What He Wanted in *Phantom of the Rue Morgue* (1954).
Above Unambiguous glances and gestures in *491*, an early movie by Vilgot Sjoman, who made the controversial *I Am Curious, Yellow* (1967).
Right Does this turn you on? Or make you a better lover? The curious genre of the sex-education film raises moral issues as well as body temperatures; the movie is *The Language of Love* (1970).

promote all manner of subterfuges and earnest explanations to justify an erotic scene not on its own merits but on 'artistic' grounds. (A lot of movie buffs manage to take this in their stride; to them the game of 'spot the justification' is all part of the fun.) I have, too, tried to remember that tastes in erotica vary wildly, and that what is acceptable to one person may be as the bottom of a parrot cage to another; or, to put it another way, one lady's deep throat may be another's great big yawn.

A further aspect worth mentioning at the outset has to do with the illustrations in the book. The point here is that the impact of a still photograph is vastly different to that of the 'living' screen. A photograph can show the anatomical perfection of beautiful people or sketchily suggest a fractional movement in a movie, but it can rarely represent the ambiance of an entire scene. Similarly, a photograph can suggest, but not show, movement. It would take an enormous number of stills to reconstruct, say, Nicholas Roeg's sequence in *Don't Look Now* in which he inter-cuts between Donald Sutherland and Julie Christie undressing to make love in the afternoon and dressing to go out to dinner.

That said, the subject of erotic movies is obviously a gift for illustration and the pictures included in the book should give pleasure in their own way. As for the text, it aims neither at Freudian analysis nor at being an apologia for sex films. I simply report on a number of patterns, beginning with all those hopeful starlets who may or may not have graced casting couches in their urgent bids for fame, but who with notable exceptions remained as handmaidens to fortune, their greatest moments spent grouped around the swimming pools of movie sets, instead of floating languidly in their own.

Above Ancient Romans let it all hang out in Fellini's *Satyricon* (1969).
Below Black on white – one of the movie world's most enduring taboos.

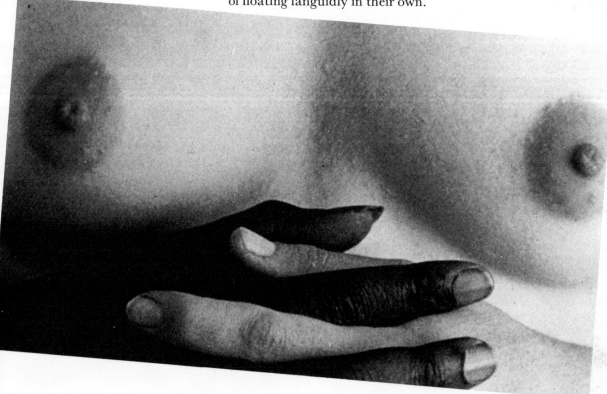

THE ATMOSPHERE PEOPLE

Previous page Underworld extras in *Dante's Inferno* (1924) at first seem near-naked, but in fact reveal tormentingly little.
Above Luxurious torpor in De Mille's *Manslaughter* (1922).
Right Claudette Colbert bathes naked in asses' milk in *The Sign of the Cross* (1932); the handmaidens rely on their décolletage and chain-appeal.
Below right Mature plus Lamarr in De Mille's *Samson and Delilah* (1949).

Eroticism to some may mean the relentless pursuit of primary erogenous zones, breasts and buttocks and that special area between the human legs where language collapses, keeling over with scientific cool or hot-rod banality. To those of a more poetic strain it could also mean secondary zones, the beauty of the eye, the length of a neck, the shape of an ankle, the smooth ardour of an armpit, the hair as curtain of the soul. Or – and this is something the cinema is unequivocally good at – it could mean, more simply, grace and energy of movement.

In the past the stronger forms of eroticism have mostly been geared to the tastes of the male consumer. However, in today's more liberated times women are no less hotly encouraged by the movie industry to join in the hunt for those not-so-elusive primary zones. Whether this enlightened policy will reap comparable dividends at the box-office is much open to doubt. In that respect I am reliably informed (at least two women have told me) that the more subtle lady still glows with sensual release at a set of well-cut fingernails, at highly polished shoes or teeth, at a male fist wrapped shyly round a bunch of forget-me-nots.

Be that as it may, here we begin with the provocative thrill of the chorus – with silent female starlets paraded in happy harems or posed round marble columns, and with muscular men sweating it out in ancient arenas pursued by lions of a non-literary nature, or swarming a-top the mainmast only to be cut down, alas, by Douglas Fairbanks or Errol Flynn.

This is, of course, the world of the movie spectacular. It is a fertile, sun-filled world receptive to the most gigantic of fantasies, a land rich in erotic incident where history has provided the warm clay for countless movie epics.

As a genre the spectacular is perhaps associated in most people's minds with America, and, more precisely, with Hollywood in the Good Old Days. Yet it would be a mistake to think only of Hollywood. Europe, too, has thrown a few orgies, motion picture-style. Today, what is more, all is not well with the American Dream Factory. It is in only moderate shape. A decade or so ago it was showing grave signs of exhaustion in, for example, the Burton-Taylor *Cleopatra* (completed in 1963 but four years in the making), and as John Huston and his zoological consultant wrestled with *The Bible* in 1966. Today the bright lights may be elsewhere. Italy's Cinecittà continues to put out a stream of neo-epics, and in Federico Fellini has the greatest showman since Cecil B. De Mille. But Fellini comes later in our story; first we go back to the early years of this century.

Epic Flesh

In the beginning, so far as movie spectaculars are concerned, were the moguls. They make a natural starting point since it was they who sired the pioneering profusions of tutu and toga that became the trademarks of the chorus. And it was they who supplied their flocks of unknown hopefuls with a special group identity, that of being the 'atmosphere people'. In this role the chorus formed an effective complement to the star actors and actresses, for while the latter provided the mystery and the close-up glamour, they the chorus added the essential background aroma, as well as the acres of flesh needed to sustain a good take at the box-office.

We begin with perhaps the most famous mogul of all, Cecil Baines De Mille (1881–1959), every inch of him a showman in his on-set costume of high boots, megaphone, breeches and revolver (the latter for dealing with over-excited lions). Bessie Love said of this extraordinary man, the ex-actor son of a would-be Episcopalian minister, that it was a pleasure to be turned down by him. Another witness found him a 'Nero' on set but 'charming and terribly appreciative' off it. De Mille did much to shape the style of the 1920s, at first with socio-sexual comedies and later with the biblical epics for which he is best remembered. He made *The Ten Commandments* twice, the first version in 1924, the second in 1956. At his death in 1959 he was planning a large look at the scouting movement entitled, unsurprisingly, *Be Prepared*. The French writer and artist Jean Cocteau called him a great naïve painter, and Paul Rotha, film critic, less flatteringly pointed in 1930 to his 'shrewd sense of the bad taste of the lower type of the general public, to which he panders, and a fondness for the daring, vulgar, and pretentious'. Reputedly De Mille's daring included arranging for his niece, Agnes, to dance naked on top of an elephant; and if that story is apocryphal, his use of the Big Cats is authenticated many times over. Lions, leopards, and at least two Bengal tigers added a sense of the exotic if not always the erotic to many a

De Mille spectacular. Their presence on set also had an undeniable effect on some of their co-stars, as witness the occasion when Victor Mature, playing Samson in *Samson and Delilah* (1948), refused to wrestle with his lion and opted for a rug instead, which he tamed in close-up whilst a stand-in took on the lion in long-shot. 'But Victor, he was raised on milk,' coaxed Cecil B. 'So was I, but I eat meat now,' said Samson.

Animals have acted out more than one sexual fantasy in the history of the spectacular. De Mille's *The Sign of the Cross* (1932) originally had a naked Christian girl offered to a gorilla; later this was changed to a couple of lions who paid no attention to the girl. (The final movie had its erotic compensations in the form of Claudette Colbert, as Nero's wife, bathing naked in 400 gallons of asses' milk.) Lions had also been a feature of an earlier film, *Male and Female* (1919), in which Thomas Meigham imagined himself as a barbarian king feeding the beasts with a princess.

It is not fashionable to praise De Mille for his art, only to envy his acute sense of what the public wanted and could be shown at any one time. In 1919, a busy year, he gave them a Grecian-style ball scene decorated with curvaceous living statues in *Don't Change Your Husband*. By 1924 he had moved on to his own brand of titillatory religion with *The Ten Commandments*; and in 1927 he came up with *King of Kings*, whose storyline suggested an eternal triangle between Mary Magdalene, Judas Iscariot and Jesus Christ.

However grand the theme, De Mille always matched its magnitude by flamboyantly boasting of the deep historical research underpinning the movie – two thousand books and periodicals were invoked, for example, to shore up *The Ten Commandments*. Fortunately, De Mille never allowed historical research to dull his imagination, and as an erotic illusionist he was formidable. In *The Story of Epic Films* John Cary pays tribute to De Mille's 'ability to involve the camera – i.e. the spectator – physically by means of dramatic editing, lushly textured backgrounds, erotic costuming and the sounds of pleasure that underscore the action'.

Even before De Mille, other filming fathers were not averse to a dash of sensuality. In France Georges Méliès, a former conjuror and one of the very first film-makers, had not only pioneered trick photography (his contemplation of the mechanism of his wife's sewing machine inspired a new form of camera), he also introduced Parisian beauties onto celluloid. His ladies appeared either singly, as in *The Brahmin and the Butterfly* (1902), in which a bathing belle flutters out of her chrysalis, or were grouped as, for example, mermaids in *Twenty Thousand Leagues Under the Sea* (1907). Méliès made literally hundreds of movies in the years before World War I. Today they seem rather heavily stage-orientated, but he is at last receiving recognition for his work. In his own time he was soon neglected, most of his negatives were sold off to manufacturers for recycling, and he spent his old age running a gift kiosk on the Gare Montparnasse. He died in 1938.

In America another pioneer, D. W. Griffith, was mainly concerned to push back the frontiers of film as an art form: this master of visual storytelling who loved the great Victorian writers gave the cinema much of its primary 'language' – his use of the close-up for significance, and the long-shot for spectacle, would by themselves have assured his place in cinematic history. In addition, he offered passion on the grand scale in *The Birth of a Nation* (1915) and was rewarded with huge box-office receipts. He then made *Intolerance* (1916) from an equally brilliant concept, but this was a financial disaster – despite some special injections of flesh ordered by the 'powers that be'. In 1964 the film's assistant director, Joseph Henabery, talked to Kevin Brownlow, author of *The Parade's Gone By*, about how he set about placating these 'powers'.

'As a basic shot I developed a section from an old painting known as *Belshazzar's Feast*. It was a wild party, I can tell you. A real orgy. I had people lying around so that they weren't stark naked – almost, but not quite . . . I didn't know it at the time but Griffith back East was shooting some naked women he'd dug up from the red-light district.'

Belshazzar's feast was celebrated in true epic style. The ramparts of Babylon rose ninety feet above the surrounding Californian suburbs, and giant stone elephants trumpeted their excitement at the drunken nude mob. Technically, too, the film contained exciting innovations, including the introduction of a crane-and-boom system which allowed the camera to swoop dramatically down and forward from the outer wall into the palace.

Above A nipple is tastefully bared before party guests in D. W. Griffith's *The Sorrows of Satan* (1926).
Left Three lightly veiled beauties form a *pose plastique* amid the wonders of *Long Distance Wireless Photography*, as the technologically minded Georges Méliès called this 1907 movie.
Below 'Figures don't lie' – demonstrated by four starlets from the Mack Sennett 'fun factory', which unflaggingly supplied the new movie magazines of the '20s with pin-up photos of aspiring actresses.
Below right Grinning in the rain – Vitaphone girls from the chorus of *Operator's Opera*.

Right A starlet who made the leap to stardom from out of a Ziegfeld chorus line – Louise Brooks, perhaps best known for her role as the tart, Lulu, in G. W. Pabst's *Pandora's Box* (1929), filmed in Germany.

Above The girls in the band; from the 1925 version of *Ben Hur*.
Left After the orgy in *Femina*.
Below A cascade of near-nudes in blond wigs spills from the gilded couch of *Casanova* (1927).
Right Chorus girls wearing knickers of generous cut maintain studied poses in *The Common Law* (1931).

Meanwhile, back among the businessmen, William Fox had accepted the advice of a Broadway producer and put an unknown actress under contract. In doing so he helped to launch the star system in America and gave the movie world its first love goddess, Theda Bara. Her principal turn comes later in our story, in Chapter 4; for now it is sufficient to place her in time – she made her first movie, *A Fool There Was*, in 1914 – and to recall David Robinson's judgment, in his book *World Cinema*, that her career output of some forty films 'established sex as the *sine qua non* of American films, with domestic intrigue, marital infidelity and the triangle drama as dominant motifs'.

The Bara craze lasted until the end of the decade – just; by the 1920s she was out of date. But for thousands of young chorus hopefuls these were more satisfying years. Among them were the Sennett girls, a popular creation of Mack Sennett's 'fun factory', who slipped into bathing suits and spent long hours skipping about among the waves along the seashore; they also perched seductively on the running-boards of automobiles. More important from an historical viewpoint, their alluring shapes were regurgitated endlessly in the pages of the new movie magazines.

In effect, the silent starlets found their public voice in the magazines, more particularly through the gossip columnists, who loved nothing more – when they weren't gargling in acid drops about the screen and private lives of the stars – than to sing the praises of the starlets and so boost their budding aspirations. Thus an issue of *Photoplay* decorated its pages with girls like Lillian Knight, a Sennett girl and also Miss Los Angeles 1924; she glistens in a sexy sheen of oil and is described as 'a high tribute in the land of Beautiful Women'. Elsewhere, an article asks the question beloved of starlets the world over. Referring to Flo Ziegfeld's girls, it says: 'Remember how many young women have stepped from the pulchritudinous precincts of the Follies to achieve glory on the screen? Olive Thomas, Marion Davies, Kay Laurel, Rubye de Remer, Jacqueline Logan, Kathlyn Perry, Shannon Day, Billy Love, Irene Marcellus . . . Which one of the Follies flappers on these pages will be silver sheet stars? We shall see.'

One Follies girl was Louise Brooks, who as a teenager had her sexy, Ziegfeld-trained walk satirized in a New York hotel by Chaplin. She graduated to silent stardom and has recently become something of a cult figure, an elegant and sharp-minded woman with the perhaps unique distinction of throwing her half-written memoirs, *Naked on My Goat*, into the incinerator.

Orgies, European Style

In the 1920s, while America set the pace for historico-biblical extravaganzas, Old Europe was, albeit on a smaller scale, master of the erotic revels. The Italians, true to the credo of their Ancient ancestors, remained unafraid of the orgy and in consequence their film-makers ran into fewer censorship problems than their American counterparts. The same horny old epic themes, Cleopatra, Quo Vadis and the rest, were explored with generous helpings of toga-tugging and naked togetherness.

The German cinema showed a similar inclination to reveal all. Titles made soon after World War I would seem at home at the rougher end of today's market, e.g. *Die Verführten* ('The Seduced'), *Hyänen der Lust* ('Hyenas of Lust') and *Das Paradies der Dirnen* ('The Whores' Paradise'). A new approach to mass nudity was proposed by Berlin's UFA studios, who made a feature-length documentary called *Ways to Health and Beauty*, in which naked star-

Left and below Germanic uplift in the UFA production *Ways to Health and Beauty*, a full-length documentary hymn to naturism that was part of a series of *Kulturfilme* made by that studio.

lets (male and female) leaped and danced and posed in praise of callisthenics against a changing background of elaborately recreated Greek gymnasia and Roman baths. In another product of the same studio, *The Secret of the Orient* (1928), the naked chorus formed more desultory patterns to match the languid plant forms of the set design which, even round the inevitable pool, exuded the exhausted air of an Eastern hothouse.

Right In a wartime film called *Freude* ('Joy'), made in 1944, or at about the time of the fall of Italy, Hitlerian Lili Marlenes stand in line on glittering plinths – as if, perhaps, in expectation of a nude motorcade, organized by their declining Führer.

In the '20s a Frenchman, Abel Gance, came to the fore as a stylish presenter of history-as-erotic-tableaux. A pioneer of the wide screen, he established himself as 'the Griffith of France'; in 1931 he made *La Fin du Monde* ('The End of the World'), whose plot revolved round a scientist's prediction that the Earth was about to be devastated by a wayward comet. With their expectations of life drastically curtailed, Gance's wealthy characters fling themselves into orgies redolent with the spirit of 'tomorrow we die'; the results so perturbed the American censors that these scenes had to be cut from their export version. Gance had a weakness for orgies. The authors of Playboy's *History of Sex in the Cinema* have this to say of a later Gance spectacular: 'His 1935 version of *Lucrezia Borgia* was replete with High Renaissance voluptuaries at their favorite pursuits – nude bathing en masse, followed by vast banquets, followed by more fun and games. The fun included a shot of one of the revelers biting the bare breast of his *inamorata*; whilst for games, Gance offered perhaps the most explicit rape scenes ever put on film. At one point a noble is seen in the very act of mounting his trembling prey.' Needless to say, *Lucrezia Borgia* came in for a re-make (in 1952) with Martine Carol luxuriating among her maidservants and some carefully posed groping among the extras.

Above left A line of Godiva figures on parade, their chest-wigs swept triumphantly aside, in the Italian epic *Theodora, Empress of Byzantium*. High above the crowd, on a narrow ledge, an intrepid 'atmosphere girl' combines with a carved bird of prey to form the image of a sphinx.

Below The orgy sequence in French director Abel Gance's *The End of the World* (1931), in which a collection of worldly characters, believing that the Earth is about to be destroyed, determine to occupy the time remaining to them with vigorous and indiscriminate love-making. These scenes upset the American censors and as a result had to be excised from the US version of the movie.

Above Renaissance voluptuaries are entertained to topless dancing in Abel Gance's *Lucrezia Borgia* (1935); like his *The End of the World*, this film also suffered badly from the American censor's knife.

Left Erotic fondling among the extras in the 1952 version of *Lucrezia Borgia*, which starred one of France's most eminent post-war Bosom Queens. Martine Carol.

Right The unkindest bite of all . . . about to be taken during an orgy sequence in Abel Gance's controversial *Lucrezia Borgia*.

Busby Berkeley and the Musical Revolution

Some of the brightest prospects for eroticism lay at this time in the sensual harmonies of the musical, in particular as created by the astonishing Busby Berkeley. Berkeley fits the over-subscribed label of genius for the breathtaking quality of his imagination. Starting with the simple chorus line, he moulded it to abstract Art Deco structures and devised countless kaleidoscopic girlie numbers to thrill the eye. He had girls playing harps made of girls in *Fashions of 1934*; Nubian slaves and harem girls in *Roman Scandals* (1933); peep-show silhouettes in *Gold Diggers of 1933* and toy trumpets lifted out of the floor to salute the legs of Ann Miller in *Small Town Girl* (1953). Alongside such scenes were the lavish waterfall numbers in *Footlight Parade* (1933), which he later echoed with Esther Williams in *Million Dollar Mermaid* (1952). The results of a Berkeley-directed sequence were nearly always staggering, and remained so throughout his long career. And yet in a 1973 interview Berkeley made the creative process seem almost simplicity itself.

For the 'No More Love' number in *Roman Scandals* the setting was a slave market. Chained girls were draped around each level of a pedestal which, he explained, 'graduated in tiers. I thought it would be a very lovely thing for the top row to be all nudes, with long blonde wigs almost down to their knees. I was going to try to photograph them nude. First I thought I would have to put flesh-lings on them of some kind. It made a striking thing with all of them chained to this block . . . I realized that if I wanted to do close-ups, that fleshlings on them would show up as being obvious; so I asked the girls if they would mind being photographed nude provided it was done in a beautiful and artistic manner by dressing their hair over their breasts, etc. They said they would do it if I would close the set and film it only at night to avoid unnecessary visitors.' And so he/they did.

The contribution of Busby Berkeley to the musical chorus line will never be surpassed. Many other musicals have had spectacular girlie scenes, such as that in *Flying down to Rio* (1933) in which the chorus takes to the air and flies, thighs braced and hair streaming, on the wings of airborne planes. But it was Berkeley who extended the role of the chorus farther than his contemporaries, endowing it with an erotic content that few before him had dreamed of, or in his own time could emulate.

Here Come the Nudies

After World War II movie screens grew bigger, even though what they had to show was not always so good. For another two decades, at least until the collapse of full-scale Hollywood, there was plenty of work for a new generation of 'atmosphere people', who found themselves valiantly replaying the sins of their forefathers. The Cleopatra movie, the Quo Vadis movie, the Spartacus, the Salome, the Sodom and Gomorrah – they did them all . . . again.

Not unnaturally, the starlet-to-star process continued to flourish. Hollywood remained the great international lure. Here it is interesting to look for a moment at the fortunes of Italy's most famous

Right The comely Jane Russell skips between a chorus line of all-male beefcake in *Gentlemen Prefer Blondes* (1953).
Below A svelte Leda appears ready to submit to an ostrich-feathered Swan in *Bal Tabarin*, a showcase spectacular featuring the famous night club in Montmartre.

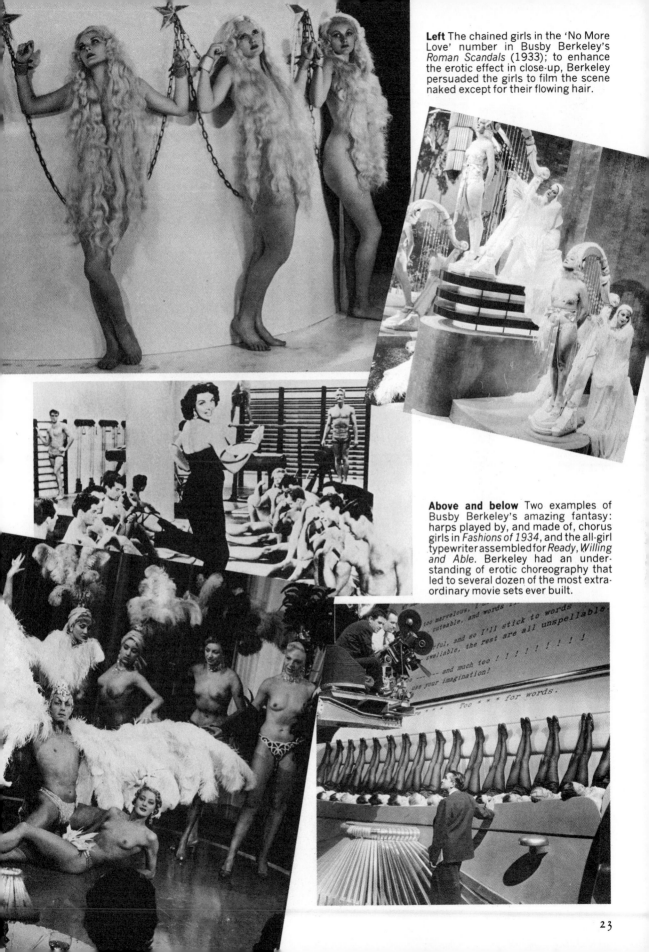

Left The chained girls in the 'No More Love' number in Busby Berkeley's *Roman Scandals* (1933); to enhance the erotic effect in close-up, Berkeley persuaded the girls to film the scene naked except for their flowing hair.

Above and below Two examples of Busby Berkeley's amazing fantasy: harps played by, and made of, chorus girls in *Fashions of 1934*, and the all-girl typewriter assembled for *Ready, Willing and Able*. Berkeley had an understanding of erotic choreography that led to several dozen of the most extraordinary movie sets ever built.

23

24

starlet-turned-star, Sophia Loren. Certainly one of the more encouraging examples of rags to riches, Miss Loren is not allowed to forget her naked beginnings in *Era Lui, Si, Si* (1951) as a barebreasted extra. In 1949 she had won second prize in a beauty competition wearing a dress made from her mamma's window curtains. Escaping from her barefoot background in the Neapolitan slums, she came to the Cinecittà in Rome. Carlo Ponti, the movie tycoon, asked her to appear in another competition for which he was one of the judges. She lost the contest but gained the judge. The rest is history. In contrast, her near-contemporary, Gina Lollobrigida, also started as a bit player in Italian epics, but 'La Lollo' then became a sex star in the old Hollywood sense of the term, making familiar-sounding movies such as *Solomon and Sheba* (1959).

When Hollywood fell into decline in the mid-'60s, under pressure from a growing TV industry and because public tastes had changed, the dimensions of the blockbuster grew considerably thinner. No longer were the 'atmosphere people' so fully employed by the big studios, and the latter's role as purveyors of acceptable nakedness passed into more aggressive hands. In the last decade the forms of movie erotica have been fashioned by three principal groups – the 'nudie' film-makers, who were busy establishing themselves in the late '50s; the American Underground, and exploiters various. The latter have moved on from making clandestine stag films to develop the growing market for 'porno chic'.

Left Sophia Loren, ripely glowing in her early days as an extra; here she appears in a scene from *Era Lui, Si, Si* (1951). By the mid-late '50s her film-producer husband, Carlo Ponti, had set her on the way to world stardom.
Below The role of the extra changed in the late '50s with the advent of 'nudie' and 'sexploitation' movies: for these low-budget titillators, willing 'atmosphere people' were thrust more and more into close-up, their bodies meshing to the strident rhythms of simulated sex. The film illustration is from *The Psycho Lover*.
Bottom Good, old-fashioned slavegirls flank Ringo Starr and Raquel Welch in *The Magic Christian* (1969).

Old-style fumbles against marble columns have become new-style group sex on the living-room carpet, or the floor of a forest clearing (see Chapter 3). Russ Meyer, responsible among his early efforts for *The Immoral Mr Teas* (1959), was a pioneer in the field of 'nudies', or 'skinflicks', in other words movies that go some way beyond the call of orthodox naturism. Not all is novelty, however, and a few recognizably old-fashioned titles persist: one such is Irv Hunsicker's *Torrid Toga* (1970), which depicted bouncy fun down at the Roman baths, ancient pursuits enacted by contemporary folk in search of wine and the warmth of an ample-breasted slavegirl.

In the Underground movement the name of Andy Warhol is probably the best known to date. His excursions into bisexual and homosexual relationships have produced, not surprisingly, some variants on the theme of group activity. In *Lonesome Cowboys* (1968) the sex angle is portrayed, in the overmodulated words of one critic, 'by showing naked cowboys under blankets together, uncoy, tough, men'. (There is more about the revelations of Warhol and his friends in Chapter 4.)

So the extras still have work to do, but the chorus line has shrunk. It is left to someone of Federico Fellini's stature to restore some of the old corrupt glories and squeeze from the grape his full-bodied taste for life – and for his own fantasies. One of his more typically epic productions was *Satyricon* (1969), which was crammed with titillating diversions practised by the nouveau-riche libertines of Nero's Roman Empire. Fortunately for the 'atmosphere people', the imagination of Fellini, a former cartoonist, cheerfully embraces all types and ages; this means that his extras can start young, learning their trade as, perhaps, delicate water-babies in yellow curls. Fellini also has a special affection for the genially grotesque, and has gallantly kept in work numerous female extras of Gargantuan size.

Once upon a time there was a movie called *The Imperial Sins of Susanna*. It was made, to be precise, in 1968, the year of the Paris students' revolt. In it Napoleon Bonaparte appears to be incapable of laughter. We learn that Susanna, the heroine, has discovered a plot against him which will have bad repercussions for the entire population of Giessen, a pretty little German town. Susanna determines a course of action. She gathers together the one hundred and twenty most beautiful girls of the district, leads them in front of the castle and, in the presence of the astonished emperor, they take off all their clothes. Napoleon laughs, loudly.

Such is the role of the erotic extra, to be both decorative and silently suggestive. She may yet end by starving at the gates of Hollywood or die under mysterious circumstances and ruin the career of a Fatty Arbuckle. She may pose that much more provocatively in the pages of movie magazines, or become a movie executive's plaything. A false mythology may surround her casting couch; but the double bed in the next chapter is not for her. This is reserved for the Star.

Previous pages Carefree chorines of the post-pubic age dance in Pasolini's *Canterbury Tales* (1972).
Above The joys of see-through fashion, vibrantly displayed in the brothel scene in Federico Fellini's *Roma* (1972).
Below Two fine specimens of Fellini's 'atmosphere people', from *Satyricon* (1969). The wild carnivals that Fellini, a former cartoonist, portrays in his films call for an unendingly rich stream of young boys, nubile girls and wondrous grotesques of either sex.
Right Perhaps the modern screen's most controversial lover is Marlon Brando: his films have regularly run into censorship trouble since the raping of Blanche (Vivien Leigh) in *A Streetcar Named Desire* (1951). Here Brando hits his mark with Stephanie Beacham in *The Nightcomers* (1971).

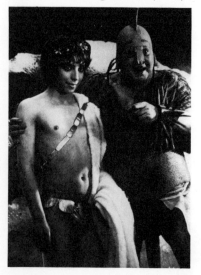

TO KISS...AND SO TO BED

The first accredited film kiss was by May Irwin and John C. Rice in a movie of the same name, Edison's *The Kiss* (1896), and as a consequence of their daring those stalwart stars have graced the pages of many an historical survey. Taken from a Broadway melodrama, *The Widow Jones*, the movie's impact would be easy to underestimate today; but we can record that in its own time it aroused high-octane reactions, drawing this immediate attack from one Herbert S. Stone, who on 15 June 1896 wrote: 'Neither participant is physically attractive, and the spectacle of their prolonged pasturizing on each other's lips was hard to bear. When only life-sized it was pronounced beastly. But that was nothing to the present sight. Magnified to Gargantuan proportions and repeated three times over it is absolutely disgusting. All delicacy or remnant of charm seems gone from Miss Irwin, and the performance comes near to being indecent in its emphasized vulgarity . . . The Irwin kiss is no more than a lyric of the Stock Yards.'

In time the erotic impact of screen kisses became less pronounced. Even so, the debate continued in various forms ranging from discussions on decency to artistic considerations. King Vidor explains in his autobiography, *A Tree is a Tree*, how Lillian Gish for the making of *La Bohème* (1926) was reluctant to embrace John Gilbert, then at the height of his romantic fame as a screen lover. 'She argued that if we photographed their lips

Left The first screen kiss, by May Irwin and John C. Rice in 1896.
Above The face as erogenous zone: Marlene Dietrich and Robert Donat in *Knight Without Armour* (1937).
Below Greta Garbo and John Gilbert in *The Flesh and the Devil* (1927).
Bottom Kiss of the whip? John Barrymore at risk in *The Tempest* (1928).

coming together in a kiss, a great amount of suppressed emotion would be dissipated. She was convinced that if we avoided this moment a surge of suppressed romance would be built up.' Lovers separated by space worried MGM producer Irving Thalberg, who ordered some judicious- re-shooting to 'bridge the gap' between Gilbert and Gish.

Theda Bara and her kohl-rimmed eyes had already opened up the era of the long kiss in 40 movies made between 1915 and 1920; while *The Sea Beast* (1925) spawned a kiss that was very much in opposition to Miss Gish and the school of modesty. In this scene John Barrymore, famous for his 'great profile' and his stage *Hamlet*, goes into an enormously long clinch with Dolores Costello. The clinch was in fact composed of four takes strung together; to publicize it, Warner Brothers spread word that Dolores had fainted in the middle of shooting the scene.

If the film star's face has always been his or her fortune, there was a time in the '20s when the face was also *the* erogenous zone, gasped at and sighed over by millions of moviegoers. It became the focus   massive in close-up – of almost every romantic climax, attended in the director's lens by muted hairstyles and flattened breasts whose intrinsic interest was kept purposefully small in order not to distract from the magic of those new principals, the eyes and lips, which were now conceived of as holding love's secrets.

In such a climate a great star like Greta Garbo soon reached the point where mere 'pasturizing on each other's lips' would no longer do. In his book *Stardom*, Alexander Walker notes the skill with which Garbo builds up an image of erotic power through a sequence of kisses. The film is *The Temptress* (1926): ' . . . she places a little flurry of kisses on Moreno's cheek, then masks his eyes with her hand as she plants a longer one on his face, blotting the vision of her out of his sight while she leaves him with a final touch of the lips'. The scene is a minor masterpiece: with a few delicate and precisely planned movements, Garbo conveys all.

By way of variety, in the following year she and another considerable star, John Gilbert, were exploring the idea of kissing and making love lying down (*The Flesh and the Devil*). The novelty (at least on the silver screen) of their efforts was strengthened by the way Garbo seems determined to assume the dominant position, the male star's head resting in her lap.

But whether the star was active or passive, the mere *sight* of him or her on the screen was undeniably arousing. As Gillian Hanson writes in *Original Skin*, the presence of 'the most beautiful animal in the world, known to all, offered to all' ensured that 'the sexual fantasy was never far from the surface'. This availability was tantamount not just to knowing but even to sleeping with the star – in the imagination, that is. And perhaps no single star of the '20s stimulated more erotic worship than Rodolpho Alphonso Raffaelo Pierre Filliberti Angelimodo Valentino d'Antonguolla.

In *Son of the Sheik* (1926) there is an exchange between Valentino and Vilma Banky which contains the essence of those remote love affairs that Valentino's female followers supposedly enjoyed with him in the turbulent surroundings of their innermost thoughts.

Vilma Banky: 'Who are you, my lord? I do not know your name.'

Valentino: 'I am he who loves you. Is not that enough?'

Before his death in 1926 at the age of 31, Valentino had unforgettably reminded a generation of the daughters of the Revolution that there was more to life than housework and doing the shopping. So much so that, as late as 1953, 50,000 women a year were still visiting his rather phallic monument in De Longpre Park, Hollywood.

Left Valentino, on the attack, gives Nita Neldi's breast an encouraging/threatening squeeze in *Blood and Sand* (1922). The Latin Lover was worshipped for his apparent refusal to take no for an answer.
Above For thirty years Cary Grant kidded and kissed a score of major Hollywood heroines. One of his early conquests in this triumph of Old World style was Mae West in *I'm No Angel* (1933).
Below Cary Grant nuzzles a path on to Ingrid Bergman's pillow in a later movie, *Notorious* (1946).

A female fan writing to *Picturegoer* in March 1923 revealed much about contemporary erogenous zones when, all-a-gush, she declared the source of the Latin Lover's appeal:

'Tis his adorable smile. With one or two exceptions all film actors' molar displays are so obviously just-that-minute-made-to-order-grin and remind one of a death's head combined with Uriah Heap. Rudy, on the other hand, makes his spontaneous, it's so half-lazy-sleepy-pathetic-humorous-tolerant-varmint-street-araby, with just a suspicion of spiciness – in truth it's a human smile.' Alexander Walker, with fewer adjectives, analyses his kissing power in two films: in *Son of the Sheik* (1926) where he drives the heroine backwards towards a bed 'like a dog cornering a sheep. His kisses are blows, not caresses'; and in the film which made him a superstar, *The Four Horsemen of the Apocalypse* (1921). Here Valentino has interrupted a couple dancing. 'Suddenly,' writes Walker, he 'beats the man to the floor with his stock whip and takes over the girl, guiding her into a lazy tango, both of them sagging sensuously then darting back and forth impulsively. He ends by pressing his mouth over hers like a suction cup.' In the seduction scene in the same film, Walker describes how he flirts over tea, 'kissing the sugar lump before he drops it into her cup, transferring a kiss by his finger-tips to her lips as if putting the stamp on some billet doux'.

Thus the screen clinch became firmly established. Of all the examples, from the tender to the tough, no one star can better express these preliminaries to passion than Cary Grant, who in a long, long career has kissed an apparently endless line of leading ladies with ageless charm and unflappable style. There was Tallulah Bankhead in *The Devil and the Deep* (1932); Marlene Dietrich in *Blonde Venus* (1932); Mae West in *She Done Him Wrong* (1933); Katharine Hepburn in *Sylvia Scarlett* (1936); Joan Bennett in *Big Brown Eyes* (1936); Jean Harlow in *Suzy* (1936); Jean Arthur in *Only Angels Have Wings* (1939); Irene Dunne in *My Favourite Wife* (1940); Katharine Hepburn again in *The Philadelphia Story* (1940), where he sets about reclaiming his former wife – a favourite motif with Grant; Ingrid Bergman in *Notorious* (1946); 'early' Marilyn Monroe in *Monkey Business* (1952); Grace Kelly in *To Catch a Thief* (1955); Deborah Kerr in *An Affair to Remember* (1957); Sophia Loren in *The Pride and the Passion* (1957); Suzy Parker and Jayne Mansfield in *Kiss Them for Me* (1957); Eva Marie Saint in *North By Northwest* (1959); Jean Simmons in *The Grass is Greener* (1960); Doris Day in *That Touch of Mink* (1962), and Audrey Hepburn in *Charade* (1963).

Cary Grant's active career spanned the Decades of the Clinch. And when the ordinary kissing, as typified by Grant, began to lose its impact, it was overtaken by saucier variants, with pecks at necks and nipples, and later at private parts. Around the late '50s the indications were that even the red lips of ever-improving colour techniques could no longer distract the emotional eye of the audience from its more bullish needs. It was time to move into the bedroom – and fail to close the door.

Codes of Misbehaviour

Most important of the rule books governing the freedom of movie-makers was the Motion Picture Production Code. This was first drafted in 1929 after rising pressures from religious bodies and the American public at large had indicated that the insouciant '20s were about to be succeeded by a period of withdrawal and moral uncertainty. The movie industry, financially beleaguered since the Wall Street Crash, decided to fall in with the national mood by exercising a formal system of self-restraint; this, it was felt, would be better than to suffer the supposed 'greater evil' of having restrictions by a government body.

In an admittedly fairly relaxed way, the movie industry in the United States was already self-censoring. One measure introduced

Once the Motion Picture Producers' Code was under way, *Look* magazine published a set of examples underlining particular transgressions.

Below 'Unusual Kisses'. No more could stars plant kisses just anywhere. Unlike Don Alvarado, here too literally necking with Lili Damita in *The Bridge of San Luis Rey* (1929), future embraces had to be restricted to the lips only.

Right 'Prostitutes'. They could only be featured if essential to the plot, and had to appear unattractive.

Below right 'Thighs'. No flesh must show between stocking-tops and underwear. The outside of a bared thigh was permitted; but the inside was taboo.

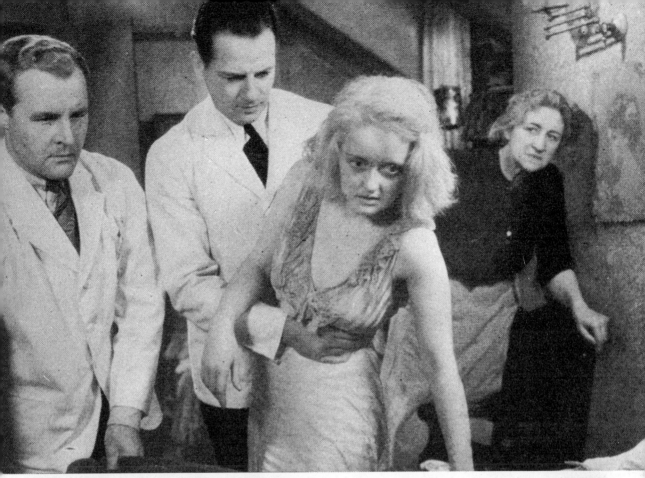

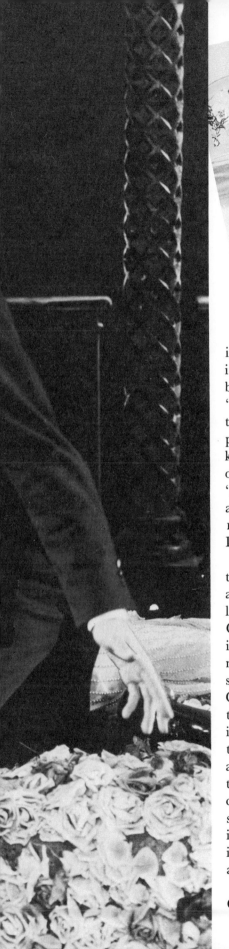

Left How to make it with one foot on the floor; from *Three Weeks* (1924).
Above William Powell and Myrna Loy, though married, had to keep to single beds in *Song of the Thin Man* (1947).

in the previous decade was a set of 'Don'ts' and 'Be Carefuls', intended as general guidelines on how particular themes should be treated. In movies dealing with crime and violence, for example, 'The use of firearms' was rated a 'Be Careful', while 'The illegal traffic in drugs' was classified 'Don't'. Similarly, in sex matters producers were reminded to 'Be Careful' of 'Excessive or lustful kissing, particularly when one character or the other is a heavy'; on the other hand, 'Any inference of sex perversion' was a 'Don't'. These instructions were issued by what became known as the Hays Office, named after its chief, Will H. Hays, who in 1922 became president of the Motion Picture Producers and Distributors of America (elsewhere referred to as the MPPA).

The final spur to a more rigid form of censorship was given by the arrival of the Talkies. They opened a new dimension for artistic expression, or verbal offence, depending on how you looked at it. The MPPA looked at it severely. The Hays Office Code was written and distributed. After a short while, however, it became apparent that the Code was being freely ignored by movie-makers, even though studio heads had officially agreed to stick by its provisions. The next moves were made by various Church bodies which threatened to organize boycotts of 'sensational' films. Since the latter were the only ones making money in those Depressed years, the movie industry was compelled to take note. The Catholic Legion of Decency was founded in 1933 and within a year some ten million Catholics had been encouraged to take arms against 'the salacious motion picture'. Schoolchildren were organized into parading with banners carrying such combative slogans as 'An Admission to an Indecent Movie is a Ticket to Hell'. The Legion also drew up its own Code, which included a C for 'Condemned' rating, and lists of current releases and their ratings were widely circulated.

Hays and his men, feeling cornered, decided to enforce the Code with greater stringency. On 15 July 1934 Joseph I. Breen was made head of Production Code Administration, and from that day all member companies of the MPPA had to have their pictures formally passed by the PCA.

Ruth Inglis writes in *Freedom of the Movies*: 'Fundamentally, the complete Code is a moralistic document. The word "moral" or its derivatives appears in it twenty-six times. Valuative terms like "sin", "evil", "bad", "right", and "good" appear frequently'. In its 'Particular Applications' (the practical part that follows the philosophizing of the 'Preamble'), the Code covered twelve subject areas. These were: Crimes against the law; Sex; Vulgarity; Obscenity; Profanity; Costume; Dances; Religion; Locations; National Feelings; Titles, and Repellent Subjects.

The Code was filled with 'good' intentions, but in its efforts to lay down comprehensive legislation it set the clock back several decades. Nudity – to take a primary taboo – was completely banned, as were 'undressing scenes' and 'dancing costumes intended to permit undue exposure or indecent movements in the dance'. As for the section on Locations, this prescribed that 'the treatment of bedrooms must be governed by good taste and delicacy' – which in turn led to the notorious banning of double beds and the rule that in love scenes involving a bed the male lover must always keep one foot on the ground.

The section on Profanity is one of the most interesting, not least for its implicit fear of the new medium, Sound. The section includes the following passage: 'No approval by the Production Code Administration shall be given to the use of words and phrases in motion pictures including, but not limited to, the following: Alley cat (applied to a woman); bat (applied to a woman); broad (applied to a woman); Bronx cheer (the sound); chippie, cocotte; God, Lord, Jesus, Christ (unless used reverently); cripes; fanny; fairy (in a vulgar sense); finger (the); fire, cries of; Gawd; goose (in a vulgar sense); "hold your hat" or "hats"; hot (applied to a woman); "in your hat"; louse; lousy; Madam (relating to prostitution); nance; nerts, nuts (except when meaning crazy); pansy; razzberry (the sound); slut (applied to a woman); S.O.B.; son-of-a; tart; toilet gags; tom cat (applied to a man); traveling salesmen and farmer's daughter jokes; whore. . . .' And in a later paragraph, inserted on behalf of the movie industry as a whole in order to protect both home and foreign consumer relations, the following words are banned: Chink, Dago, Frog, Greaser, Hunky, Kike, Nigger, Spig, Wop, Yid.

The Code was repeatedly revised and amended, but in substance it remained the Code of 1934 until about 1960; in that decade its powers were progressively eroded by a flood of taboo-busting movies, one of the most notable being *Who's Afraid of Virginia Woolf* (1967).

Right In the early '50s a double shooting was needed for the massage scene in *The Secrets of Venus*. For those countries that forbade naked breasts and bottoms, the masseuse shifted sides and blocked the view.
Far right In all advertisements for the British film *Naturist Paradise*, Anita Lowe was dressed by the censor in large rectangular patches.

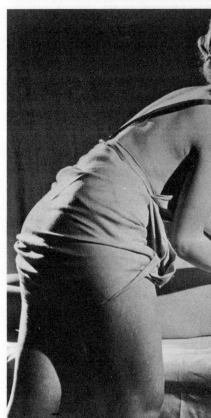

This page Brigitte Bardot and Sean Connery rehearse their moves for an outdoor love scene in *Shalako* (1968). Mlle Bardot's priceless knees are protected from the rocky ground by a studio blanket.

Right First of four colour pages featuring stars of the erotic cinema: No. 1 is Brigitte Bardot.

This page Two champions of style: Carole Lombard, luxuriously elegant, top, and Jean Harlow, more earthy, the star who shed her bra and brought the bosom back into favour after the advent of the Talkies, when words had begun to strip the face of its erotic interest.

Previous pages and left Stars of the erotic cinema: Gina Lollobrigida, at her most appealing in black lingerie; Jeanne Moreau, showering in *Chère Louise* (1972); and Sophia Loren, bedding with Marcello Mastroianni in *Sunflower* (1970).

Love's Cockpit

Even in more repressive times than our own the screen bed was never required to be entirely absent. Thus Code-bound Hollywood could feature beds but at the same time had to circle round them with caution, using 'flirt's eyes' and relying on implication and a variety of devices, of which humour was a prominent one. For example, in *It Happened One Night* (1934), Frank Capra had the problem of dealing with a pair of unmarried lovers. Claudette Colbert is a runaway heiress and Clark Gable the newspaperman assigned to track her down. In the course of the plot they are forced to share the same room in a motel. Capra resolved this by providing two beds with a blanket between them which Gable erects and dubs 'the walls of Jericho' (there was a boom in the sale of twin beds during the 1930s, thanks to the movies). The 'walls' are left standing, but at the end of the film, the couple, now married, return to the same motel and the same room. A toy trumpet is heard in the middle of the night, to the surprise of the staff. The walls have come tumbling down!

Another source of erotic comedy came in the ample shape of Mae West, she of the figure that was said to have 'launched a thousand hips' and a classic line in breezy camp, e.g. 'Is that a pistol in your pocket or are you just pleased to see me?' After entering movies rather late at approaching forty, this fearless ex-music hall comedienne caused havoc among the would-be censors with *I'm no Angel* (1933) and subsequently she became the victim of a purity campaign mounted by the eccentric Press baron William Randolph Hearst. But Mae West had resilience and survived in her self-appointed role as a walking spoof of Hollywood morality. Her speciality was verbal titillation, and she kept spirits high with her quips, e.g. 'I used to be Snow White but I drifted', her slogans, e.g. 'A thrill a day keeps the chill away', and with song titles such as 'I Wonder Where My Easy Rider's Gone'. But she also knew how to send up the baroque beds on which she sometimes sprawled: even though short in the leg – she was only 5 feet 3 inches tall – Mae West was deep in the cleavage at $43\frac{1}{4}$ inches.

Eroticism has always contained the promise of BED, and even today headlines like 'Which Hollywood Stars Sleep in the Nude?' have a sure pulling power. And to some extent the fortunes of Hollywood stars, at least in the so-called Golden Years before World War II, depended on their ability to appeal to the erotic expectations of their public. This could be done either off or on the screen, but both was preferable. Indeed, a racy private life was considered almost indispensable (Garbo being about the only one who did dispense with it). Of the early stars Gloria Swanson lived luxuriously in a penthouse on top of the Hotel Park Chambers in Manhattan and on a country estate; she bathed in black marbled bathrooms that were fitted with gold taps (bathroom scenes figure largely in movies as preludes to bed). Clara Bow liked to shoot down Sunset Boulevard in her open Kissel with seven red chows to match the colour of her hair –

demonstrating as she whizzed along the sexuality of speed, and the allied, though unspoken, promise of a fast romance. Pola Negri, an exotic plant from Poland and director Ernst Lubitsch's favourite star, reportedly slept in the nude with a revolver under her bed, introduced painted toenails to Hollywood and by her vampish body-flaunting encouraged her audiences to fantasize all manner of erotic adventures. Later came Jean Harlow, who laid the foundations of the bosom cult after the Talkies had arrived, and words had begun to strip the face of its erotic interest.

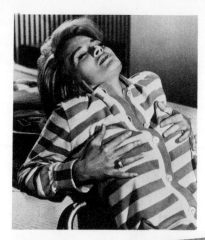

So much, then, for bedroom eyes and other erotic preliminaries. We turn now to what happens on the bed itself. Strangely, perhaps, there is no straightforward graph to be drawn, beginning with, say, the mild adventures of *The Perils of Pauline* (1914) and progressing upward to, for instance, the multiple connections unflaggingly displayed in *College Girls*, a representative 'nudie' short of the late '60s. Furthermore, although bedroom scenes are more explicit today, this is not to say that their erotic content is any higher. Eroticism corresponds as much to ideas as to appearances. Certainly too, the earlier movies were perfectly able to arouse the contemporary audiences for whom they were expressly made.

As for plots and settings, these have changed very little, while screen lovers range timelessly from the young and gentle – Dustin Hoffman and Mia Farrow in *John and Mary* (1969) – to the old taunted by the young – Frederic March by Gloria Grahame in *Man on a Tightrope* (1953) – to the lonely masturbator – Anne Heywood in *The Fox* (1968) – to lesbian embraces. The latter situation, an obligatory number in modern sex cinema, also appeared in less overt forms in the early days, enacted for example by Clara Bow in *Hoopla* (1933), and more modestly by Anita Page and Bessie Love in *Broadway Melodies* (1928). More timeless still is the constant demand for movies in which the boy-meets-girl situation is developed in more or less familiar images of poetry-in-motion – the boy lying on top of the girl until her bared teeth and misting eyes relax after orgasm into a vision of contentment.

For the male chauvinists of the world, and perhaps also a few part-time sadists, no account of the cinema's erotic mythology would seem complete without mentioning the numberless and often nameless conquests of James Bond. Bond, as the whole world must know, is a British spy created by ex-Lieutenant Commander Ian Fleming of Naval Intelligence. On his screen début, Bond was played by Sean Connery; later Roger Moore took over. Bond's first major sexual encounter was with Ursula Andress, who rises from the sea in *Dr No* (1962). His last at the time of writing was with Britt Ekland in *The Man with the Golden Gun* (1975). Other bedmates have included several enchanting Japanese actresses; Claudine Auger in *Thunderball* (1965), and the unfortunate Shirley Eaton, who in *Goldfinger* (1964) is found dead upon Bond's bed, her whole body painted in gold leaf, her skin unable to breathe. (He didn't do it.)

OLD LOVE, NEW LOVE

Top left The lone woman, Angie Dickinson in *Point Blank* (1968).

Top centre Tender love, Mia Farrow and Dustin Hoffman in *John and Mary*.

Top right Old-fashioned banditry, Douglas Fairbanks Jr and Alice Jans in *Parachute Jumper* (1932).

Centre left The fiercely simulated orgasm, Susan Strasberg and Lars Bloch in *The Sisters* (1969).

Above Lesbians of yesteryear, Clara Bow and Minna Gombell in *Hoopla* (1933).

Left Lesbian cunnilingus of last year, Sylvia Kristel on Marika Green in *Emmanuelle* (1974).

47

MORE ABOUT KISSING
Here are some kisses the Code would have hated – and in some cases did!

Right Passionate lipwork from Ali Magraw and Steve McQueen in *Getaway* (1972).

Far right, top Inventive pecking by Mai Zetterling on Tyrone Power in *Seven Waves Away* (1957).

Far right, centre A saturnine lady, only literally long in the tooth, goes for the jugular in *Vampyr Tänzerinnen* (1911).

Far right, bottom Even blacks are allowed to do it, Fred Williamson and Teresa Graves in *Black Eye*.

Centre, bottom Lesbian courtesies in von Stroheim's *The Merry Widow* (1925).

Below Contemporary necking in *Eden and After* (1970).

The Bedrooms of France

Whatever the prowess of such energetic Anglo-Saxon heroes, the mistress of eroticism and queen of the crumpled sheet is, as ever, France. Viewed as a national achievement, her record of sensual gifts would be remarkable enough even without the obvious landmarks of the Surrealist movement, the camerawork of Clouzot and Chabrol, the body worship of Martine Carol and Brigitte Bardot, the acting talent of Jean Gabin and Yves Montand, the publicity nose of Roger Vadim. What has rarely faltered is the sheer quality of France's top directors.

In 1946 Claude Autant-Lara made a tragic love-story set in World War I, *Le Diable Au Corps*, starring Gérard Philipe and Micheline Presle as the teenage schoolboy in love with an older,

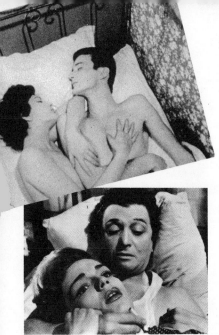

Left Jeanne Moreau and Jean-Marc Bory in *Les Amants* (1959).
Top Agnès Varda's lovers in *L'Opéra Mouffe* (1958).
Above Post-war Realism with a capital ARRRGGH! Simone Signoret's breast is assaulted with a lighted cigarette in *Dédée d'Anvers* (1947).
Below The glamorous Martine Carol in *Caroline Chérie* (1950).
Below left Brigitte Bardot at right angles with Jean-Louis Trintignant ir *And God Created Woman* (1956).

married woman. In 1958 and 1959 two other films arrived that were to influence style and technique in the making of bed scenes – respectively Alain Resnais' *Hiroshima Mon Amour* and Louis Malle's *Les Amants*. All three movies lent a poetic force to the treatment of human passion – which is what eroticism is all about. To discuss body angles or debate the amount of nudity in the pictures would cheapen the argument. All three were intense hymns to carnal knowledge, Resnais' film being visually a little more adventurous, showing life and death intertwined, opening with a close-up collage of the two naked lovers – the French actress and the Japanese businessman – on a bed where their skins glisten beneath a mica-like layer of atomic dust, their thoughts on the holocaust interspersed with the actual event.

The French, with or without their 'New Wave', produced a remarkable school of Gallic rapture in the post-war period: swimming before the eyes of an excited public came a host of feverish images ranging from historical bawdy to social realism, from sexual symbolism to lyrical escapism. *La Ronde* (1950, directed by Max Ophuls) added a sense of the wittily amoral to France's established reputation for 'Continental sophistication'; while most of that country's female stars – let alone her starlets – were prepared to display their breasts to erotic effect. There was the glamorous Martine Carol, who first came to fame with *Caroline Chérie* (1950) and was known as the 'cleanest actress in the world' because of her countless film baths; Jeanne Moreau, a topless monarch in *La Reine Margot* before her telling performance in *Les Amants* (1959), and Simone Signoret who had a cigarette end stubbed between her breasts in *Dédée d'Anvers* (1947) – that's post-war social realism for you! There was, too, Danielle Darrieux, and Simone Simon, even the beautiful Francoise Arnoul who revealed one breast to Fernandel in *Forbidden Fruit* (1952).

But the girl to outpoint them all was, of course, Brigitte Bardot. Her incredible, if simple, eroticism is to my mind best suited to the outdoor, St Tropez way of life that she, as we look back, seems almost to have invented. Accordingly, she is discussed at greater length in Chapter 3 ('The Great Outdoors'). However, it would be somewhat naïve to pretend that in her movies BB has not played some memorable bed scenes, toying with a sheet as expertly as she does with a beach towel. She was specially memorable in the bedrooms of *And God Created Woman* (1956) and *La Vérité* (1960).

One consequence of France's erotic knowhow is that the scent of French finesse has drifted across the work of film-makers in other countries, enhancing such mediocre works as the showbiz saga *Valley of the Dolls* (1967), in which Sharon Tate is hired by a 'French' director to make erotic bedroom movies. And in another overladen film, *Girl on A Motorcycle* (1968), Alain Delon, the French actor, added considerable force to his heroine's erotic fancies, clutching her naked breasts whilst she, played by Marianne Faithfull, clutched at the bed rail behind her head.

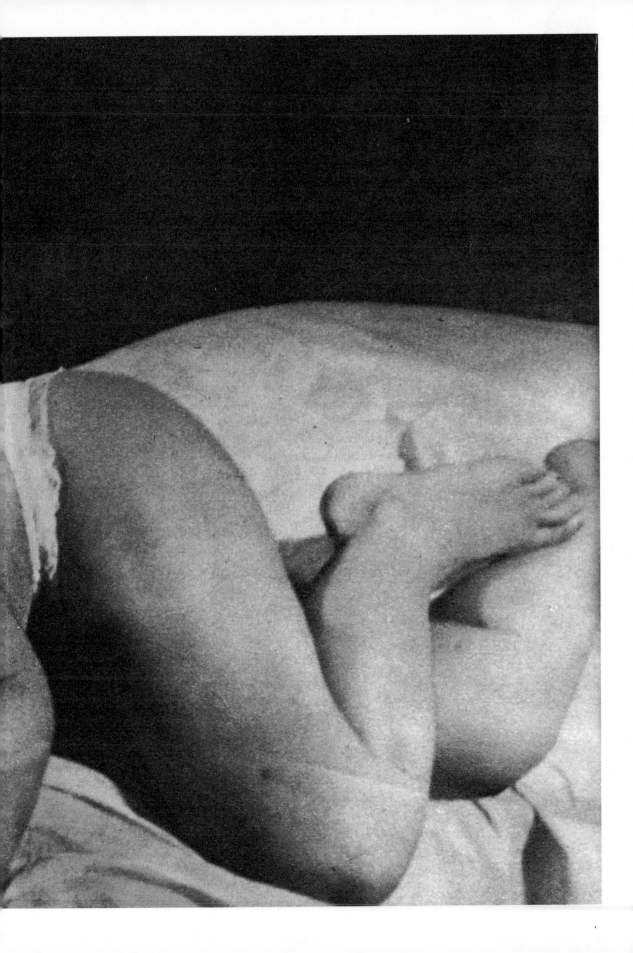

The World Loosens Up

American cinema played it safe in the bedroom until the Code relaxations of the late '60s. Nevertheless, bedroom behaviour was not ignored, and within carefully defined limits it was explored in mainstream 'sex comedies'. These catered for the great American audience of married women, with scripts tending to give the male lead some kind of come-uppance at the end – all of which has no doubt helped to preserve America's status as a matriarchy. Not that the squabbles of Doris Day and Rock Hudson, or even the edgy pair bonds of Neil Simon's scripts, added much of a bushy tail to the bright eye of our sexual theme. Occasionally, however, in a genre helped considerably by the superb acting of Jack Lemmon, the bedroom has taken on an erotic significance of its own. *The Apartment* (1960) finds Lemmon in his usual underdog role, this time as a New York office clerk who rents out his apartment to his bosses for their illicit affairs. Less typically, in *Under the Yum-Yum Tree* (1964), he plays a part lucidly described by Alexander Walker in *Sex and the Movies* as 'the lecherous landlord of Centaur Apartments which he rents only to young women, retains a key for every front door and has his own guest room papered in blood red, furnished with a double bed the size of a small yacht and equipped with automated

violins'. Despite the urgency of the decor, the erotic appeal of the movie is slight. As with most Lemmon movies, the comedy's the thing.

An erotic revolution was nevertheless on the way. And by the early '70s, kisses, however long, and beds as well, were in danger of getting swallowed down the all-capacious throat of Miss Linda Lovelace. The Continent did its best to retain its hold on sensual charm. A boy and a girl, for instance, go to bed in Milos Forman's *A Blonde in Love* (1965) but the boy has trouble with the blind, which keeps rolling up. He gets out naked to try and adjust it. It is a small moment, but touchingly funny and, in a wider sense, a moment that fills us with relief that screen lovers no longer have to keep their underwear on. In Jiri Menzel's *Closely Observed Trains* (1967) another young hero, second assistant station master, is happily cured of premature ejaculation in what used to be described as a 'frank love scene'; and in another joyful moment a willing secretary has her bare bottom authorized with the official railway stamp. France, to some extent shaken from the top of the tree of Eros, tried injections of lesbian passion to restore her position, e.g. in *Thérèse and Isabelle* (1969), and later re-doubled her efforts in *Emmanuelle* (1974). But the competition was getting heavier.

Previous pages Mylène Demongeot, expanding the '50s taste for sex kittens.
Far left, above Rock Hudson, veteran of the American sex comedy, looking older but saucier in Vadim's *Pretty Maids All in a Row* (1971).
Far left, below Jack Lemmon, a master of comedy, dubious among the tarts in *Irma La Douce* (1963).
Above Aerial nude with chandelier (*and* flames *and* skeleton) in a typically overcharged scene from *The Seven Deadly Sins*.
Left More aerobatics, from *Turkish Delight* (1973), with Rutger Hauer and Monique van de Van sharing the risks.
Below Promise of a magic carpet ride in *Chiens dans la Nuit* (1973).

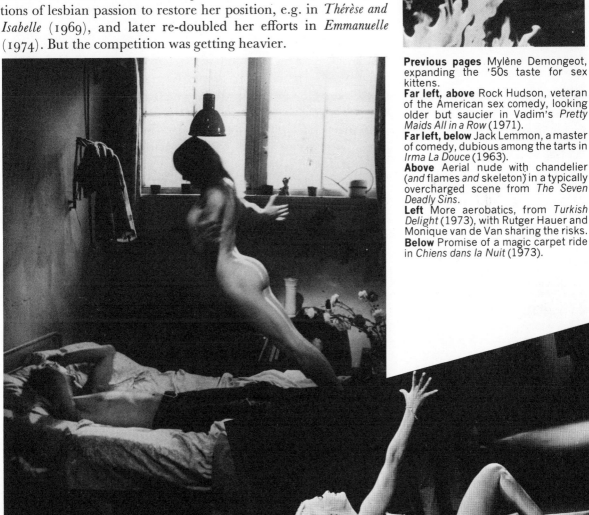

American movies were filling their beds with more than two. The partner swapping in *Bob and Carol and Ted and Alice* (1969) evolved into a trendier and cheaper form of satire in *The Telephone Book* (1974), in which Sarah Kennedy (yes, she *is* distantly related) is fascinated by an obscene telephone caller and sets out to discover his identity. En route, she finds herself auditioning for a stag film, naked with many others on a very large bed indeed.

If people tired of the bed, there was always the floor: Marlon Brando and Maria Schneider tried it and, for good measure, the butter tactic as a prelude to sodomy in *Last Tango in Paris* (1972). And in an earlier, but no less hotly debated, movie the starlets of *Blow Up* (1966) giggle and undress David Hemmings and each other on the floor of his photographer's studio.

Such tactile endeavours are not always necessary to eroticism, however. Sounds and words also have a part to play. And while the bed is undoubtedly a powerful *visual* symbol of the love force, in one of its strongest, if macabre, 'performances', it was never seen at all, only heard. This was in Polanski's *Repulsion* (1965), where Catherine Deneuve as the neurotic young hairdresser is driven frantic by the sounds of creaking springs and the gasps and moans of two lovers in the next room.

Above A new avenue in the skin trade was opened by Linda Lovelace in the still widely banned *Deep Throat* (1972); she plays the heroine for whom sex is a dull business until she discovers that her clitoris is situated in her throat.
Below The start of the studio romp in Antonioni's *Blow Up* (1966): David Hemmings watches as Jane Birkin and her fellow groupie wrestle and strip among a pile of clothes on the floor.
Below right Lovers at work in the Warhol Factory's *Blue Movie* (1969); in some quarters this film is known by an alternative title, *F**k*.
Far right Urbane jungle sirens in *Savages* sustain the Tarzan-inspired myth that sex grows on trees.

Finally, in *Ulysses* (1967) Molly Bloom, alone in her bed, speaks her mind. Her twenty-minute interior monologue, so skilfully uttered by Barbara Jefford in true Joycean language, gave heartburn to the censors. Molly's whirling mind was all too conscious of sex. 'Please delete,' said the censor, among many other lines, 'I wouldnt mind taking him in my mouth if nobody was looking as if it was asking you to suck it so clean and white he looked with his boyish face I would too in ½ a minute even if some of it went down what its only like gruel or the dew theres no danger besides hed be so clean compared with those pigs of men I suppose never dream of washing it from 1 years end to the other the most of them only thats what gives the women the moustaches I'm sure . . .'.[1]

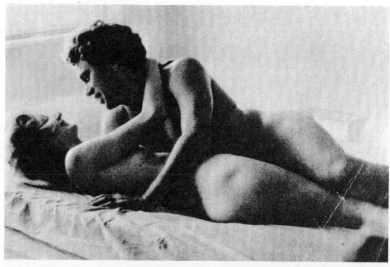

[1]From John Trevelyan's WHAT THE CENSOR SAW (1973). Britain's Greater London Council finally gave the film an X certificate.

THE GREAT OUTDOORS

In 1973, the British magazine *Films and Filming* interviewed the Italian movie-maker Franco Zeffirelli about *Brother Sun, Sister Moon*, a study he had made of St Francis. For the lead part he had taken a young English actor, Graham Faulkner, from his second term in drama school. At one point in the film Faulkner as Francis divests himself of his clothes and stands naked in the open air. 'He did it for a marvellous ideal,' explained Zeffirelli, 'to establish in front of everybody that he was giving up everything.' The hardy young actor went on to endure walking barefoot in the snow and pouring rain for twenty days, not to mention tonsuring his hair. But then came the poppies. Zeffirelli recalled. 'We were so lucky to get the best moments of creation around us. Landscapes – blooming of flowers – passing of clouds – sunsets that you couldn't believe were true. We didn't have to go to Australia or New Zealand or Canada, because it was all there twenty miles from Rome. The field of poppies looks as if we had planted billions of them specially, but it was right behind my hotel room.'

Zeffirelli's words reflect something of that sensuality which is a joy to poets and which belongs to the gentler side of eroticism. This is one aspect of nature. By contrast, in a stronger, less lyrical mood, nature can emit a considerable erotic force. We all know of the sexual symbolism of waves and waterfalls, and of the passion represented by a blood-red sun rising on a desert horizon. David Lean showed the latter in *Lawrence of Arabia* (1962); and four years later he memorably captured the impact of burgeoning spring in *Dr Zhivago* (1966) – even though, such are the necessities of art, his nodding daffodils had to come from thousands of miles away, rather than from behind his hotel room.

Perhaps, too, it is characteristic of the Great Outdoors that it can bring all five senses more powerfully into play. Thus, during the erotic grappling of Burt Lancaster and Deborah Kerr on the shore in that classic moment in *From Here to Eternity* (1953), one becomes more sensitive to the feel of the sand, the taste and smell of the salt spray and the sea breezes – as well as hearing the

Top Burt Lancaster and Deborah Kerr in *From Here to Eternity* (1953).
Centre Beach strip with spectator in

Last Day of Summer, from Poland.
Bottom St Francis steps out, in *Brother Sun, Sister Moon* (1973).

crash of the waves. All play a part in building up the atmosphere of the scene; and later the waves take over as a symbol of sexual intercourse. Such crescendoes were of course rare in 1953, and part of the scene's strength stemmed from the sight of the trim Miss Kerr, hitherto wrapped up in well-bred roles, being allowed to unleash her emotions to such an extent. In this she was also backed by a firm plotline that made her life-proclaiming love scene stand in sharp relief against the surrounding presence of the death force, war.

Undoubtedly, too, the Great Outdoors can give that extra texture to the erotic moment: one can think, for instance, of the grains of sand on the bare back of a Japanese girl in *Woman of the Dunes* (1964); of the sweat on the spilling breasts of a peasant, Vera Clouzot, as she sweeps a courtyard (*The Wages of Fear*, 1953), and of the snow on the faces of the heroines of *Women In Love* (1969). Those are just a handful of moments. There are thousands more, and yet certain images of sensuality, caught in a single frame, have become immortal. Some examples: Silvana Mangano, up to her calves in water among the women who harvest the rice crops of the Po Valley (*Bitter Rice*, 1951); James Dean, biting the earth in *East of Eden* (1955); Vivien Leigh, running the soil through her fingers in *Gone with the Wind* (1939); Kim Novak, dancing slowly on the grass with William Holden in *Picnic* (1955), and Brigitte Bardot, stalking petulantly across the beach in *And God Created Woman* (1956).

Here we may justifiably pause awhile, for in mentioning a Bardot scene we have introduced a star whose whole life, on and off screen, could seem a long-running advertisement for the Great Outdoors. In *And God Created Woman* she plays a wanton newlywed who, saddled with an inexperienced husband teases her brother-in-law into ripping off her clothes on good mother earth and 'taking' her.

Since those days she has become *the* outdoor pin-up, her down-to-earth eroticism adopted by the young and the middle-aged alike, especially in America, where *And God . . .* earned $4 million, after being relatively much less successful in France. Every remotely appropriate adjective has attended her anatomy, and the telephoto lenses of eager journalists still poke hopefully from neighbouring sand dunes in the Midi, waiting to catch the real-life sex goddess at one of her bare-breasted splashes in the sea. Her durability is much commented on ($35-23\frac{1}{2}-35$) and superbly attested by some waterside nude studies taken by her young lover for her fortieth birthday. Bardot, BB, France's most alluring visible export, she is the sapling-legged Venus de Milo to a generation whose sexual autonomy is only now emerging on a universal scale (thanks also to the Pill). She recently said: 'I live my whole life around my man – work, play, dreams, everything. My lover is the centre of my existence. When I am alone I am lost . . . Some actors say they can only really exist when they are playing a role; me, I can only play a role – only exist – when I am loved.' You are, BB, you are!

Left Swedish lyricism with Margit Carlqvist in *The Summer Wind Blows*.
Above The lovers in *One Summer of Happiness*, also from Sweden.

Above Breast appeal in *Monika – the Story of a Bad Girl*.
Right Movie poster art with, top left, Clark Gable taking his vampire stance before Vivien Leigh for the poster of *Gone With the Wind* (1939); the lettering was added separately. At bottom left is Marlene Dietrich in *Song of Songs* (1933), and on the right is the emotive central image used in the poster for *Soldier Blue* (1970).

Water Babes

The Great Outdoors in its many moods provides metaphors and realistic settings for movies ranging in character and atmosphere from lyrical Swedish to muscular American, and from nudie sexploitation to those earnest documentaries about 'the natives' that in their day were the best excuse for exhibiting the naked human form outside the pages of the *National Geographic Magazine*.

To begin with the lyrical: it was a group of Swedish filmmakers who broke the spell of post-war austerity with movies that dared to feature nude bathing scenes. They were set amid the lakes and islands of the Stockholm archipelago. This phase is usually represented in film lore with stills from *One Summer of Happiness* (1951); made by Arne Mattsson, it tells the story of a young farm girl who enjoys a brief illicit summer romance that is abruptly terminated by her death in a motor-cycle accident. The 'sylvan skinny dip' (as Playboy's *History of Sex in the Cinema* irreverently calls it) became a great cliché of the time, so much so that Christina Schollin in *Raggare*, rowing her lakeside boat alone, manages to vary the treatment by just taking off her clothes because it's a sunny day; she *doesn't* dive in. And when a man and a girl wade out naked into the water in *I Rok och Dans*, a subtitle ironically explains that the scene is 'for export'.

Overleaf Scenes from the Great Outdoors with Jane Birkin in *Projection Privée* (1973); and Sirpa Lane and Mathieu Carriere, afloat in *La Jeune Fille Assassinée* (1975).
Page 64 Marilyn Monroe with Don Murray in *Bus Stop* (1956).

60

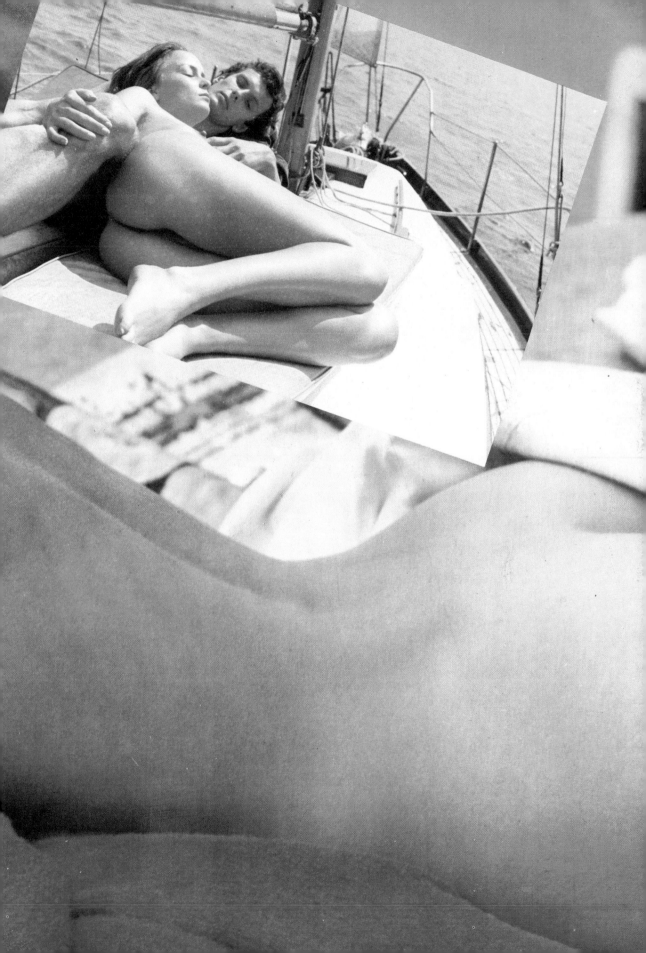

However, first prize for waterside encounters, in terms of the global ripples and *frissons* it caused, must go to *Extase* (1933), the avant-garde, rather slow Czech film by Gustav Machaty whose original title was reputedly changed from *Symphony of Love* to *Extase* because that was what the French audience shouted when they saw it in Paris.

The plot is the popular one of an old man and his young wife who is sexually unsatisfied. She, played by a very young Hedy Lamarr, swims naked in a secluded lake, hears a horseman approaching and dashes back for her clothes. Too late, the horseman has got there first. She succumbs to the charms of this stranger and her husband commits suicide. Miss Lamarr's real-life husband, Fritz Mandel, a millionaire munitions tycoon, was made of sterner stuff. He tried to buy up all the prints – not for shows down at the factory but to destroy them. In *75 Classics of the Foreign Film*, Parker Tyler says that the camera, handled 'somewhat like a voyeur, but more like an aesthete, thrilled body and soul by having stumbled on a lady who has just undressed for a dip in the water.' Hedy Lamarr says, in her autobiography *Ecstasy and Me*, that the scene was shot 'off-the-cuff' in a forest lake outside Prague, and that she had not known she was expected to appear nude. As for the 'ecstasy' that followed, 'I was told to lie down with my hands above my head while Aribert Mog whispered in my ear, and then kissed me in the most uninhibited fashion. I was not sure what my reactions would be, so when Aribert slipped down and out of camera, I just closed my eyes.' The director tried to improve on that reaction by sticking a pin in her buttock. 'The truth is that some of those pinpricks shot pain through my body until I was vibrating in every nerve. I remember one shot when the camera caught my face in a distortion of real agony, and the director yelled happily, "Yes! Good!"' So much for the adventures of a 16-year-old star. As for the film's public acceptance, that took a little longer. In the USA the Customs Bureau finally admitted it, but it was then banned in many individual cities.

In the depressed '30s people seemed to forget that outdoor eroticism had already been around for quite a while. Prominent in the early years was Annette Kellerman, an Australian dancer and swimming star, who pioneered the one-piece bathing suit and appeared in two silent Hollywood movies, *Neptune's Daughter* (1914) and *Daughter of the Gods* (1916). William Fox, who was never afraid of a little publicity, had apparently also persuaded her to appear without her one-piece. *Photoplay*, in August 1916, produced a review for *Daughter of the Gods* which has a very familiar ring to it: 'From time to time producers have used nakedness as diversion or attraction, but Brenon has made a perfectly logical use, not of nakedness but of nudity. Brenon's exquisite star and galaxy of ham mammettes quite properly wear – nothing. And you are not shocked.' Well, to be charitable, one could call it nudity of a kind, even if there *were* plenty of Lady Godiva tresses to maintain decorum.

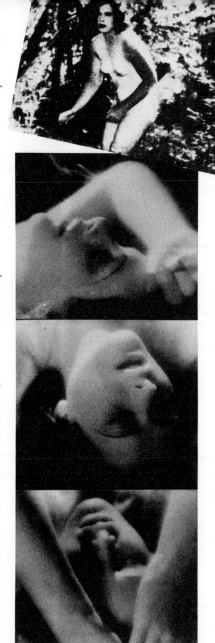

Above Hedy Lamarr, startled in the woods, then orgasmic in *Extase* (1933). **Below** Australian swimming star and underwater dancer Annette Kellerman, in *Daughter of the Gods* (1916).

Charioteers and Junglemen

On the masculine front at this time, Douglas Fairbanks Snr revealed more than mere high spirits in *The Half Breed* (1916); and although the more familiar image of him is probably that of a dashing and more thickly clad Robin Hood or Dumas Musketeer, his fabulous torso was never absent for long, glistening memorably in, for example, *The Thief of Baghdad*. (1924). Fairbanks was one of the founders of United Artists, which made William Fox one of his Hollywood rivals; Fox, of course, was determined not to be out-goosepimpled in the torso game, and on the set of *Island of Desire* he was heard to give these rousing orders to his star, George Walsh. 'Strip down, boy. We're going to show the world how a real he-man looks – all skin and whipcord!'

In 1926 Hollywood made its first big-time version of *Ben Hur*. Filming began with George Walsh in the star part, but he was then replaced by the Mexican actor Ramon Novarro. Hoping for another Valentino (he died that year), MGM trumpeted the new man's physical *and* spiritual pulling power, announcing: 'He has the body of Michelangelo's *David* and the face of an El Greco don.' To emphasize the former, a well-circulated publicity still showed him stripped and chained to an oar. We are back with a vengeance to Eros-with-energy, those well-tried ingredients of the movie spectacular. It is intriguing, too, that Lew Wallis's best-selling novel depended for its movie successes, in both this version and in the 1957 re-make, on the quality of its two setpieces, the battle at sea and the chariot race. Epic flesh wins again!

In another arena, in 1935, Willis O'Brien's outstanding trick photography helped to create a vast amount of pulsating, audience-grabbing activity during *The Last Days of Pompeii*; the film included sensual moments at the school for gladiators, an earthquake and the subsequent collapse of an enormous statue of Mars. O'Brien was having an inspired period: two years earlier (1932–33), he had contrived to create and destroy a still more bizarre yet sympathetic colossus, King Kong, and in so doing he produced one of the cinema's most alarmingly sexy images, the all-too-naked limbs of Fay Wray wriggling helplessly in the hand of the gorilla. (In this scene she is abetted though not aided by the throbbing music of Max Steiner.)

The Great Outdoors provided the stamping ground for a seemingly unbreakable chain of brawny heroics, performed by the smooth-muscled gods of the silver screen. One hero of the outdoor life who ran a veritable marathon of popularity did so in the company of a chimpanzee, a woman and a boy. Tarzan. He lives still, travelling energetically by vine across the TV screens of the world in specially written episodes (though Jane, regrettably, has been struck from the jungle lists).

Edgar Rice Burroughs invented the deep-chested yodeller in 1911. At the time ERB had not fared well, either as a door-to-door salesman, an Oregon miner or a railroad cop. Then, in

Above In the beginning was the Great Outdoors...a message firmly grasped by various moguls who foresaw the primeval loincloths of *Adam and Eve* turning to gold at the box office.
Below One of the most memorable images of the cinema: Fay Wray wriggles vainly in the determined clutch of *King Kong* (1932-33).
Left Marion Michael, erotically netted on the shoulders of the Teutonic hunter in *Liane, Forest Girl*. In the '50s Marion Michael was chosen from 11,800 applicants for the role of Liane, an athletic, golden-skinned jungle girl, conceived as a female answer to Tarzan. In real life this white goddess of the steaming forests was the daughter of a German shipping magnate; her agreeable body became the life force of a series of Liane movies.
Overleaf More trouble with the tourists: Marion Michael struggles on the straw in another scene from her forest epic, originally entitled *Liane, Mädchen aus dem Urwald*.

L-22

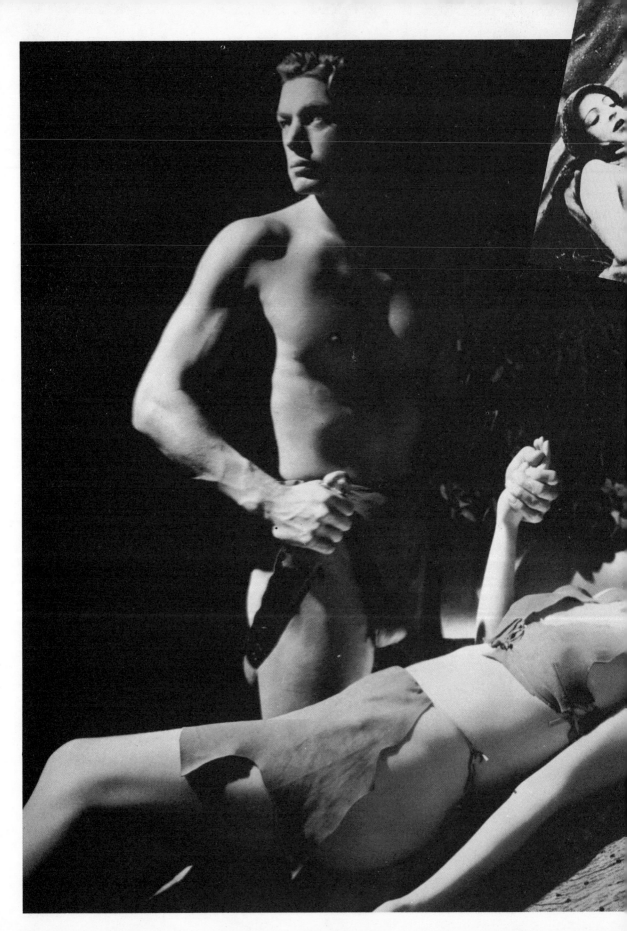

October 1912, Tarzan (the word was ape-talk for 'white skin') hit the public for the first time in *All Story Magazine*; before long, ERB's income from comic strips alone amounted to $5,000 a month. The first Tarzan movie followed in 1918.

There have been many film Tarzans, but the best known is undoubtedly Johnny Weissmuller, already famous as a swimming champion before he took the role in 1932. He had previously broken a string of records at the Olympic Games of 1924 and 1928. In the great popular tradition of these matters, Weissmuller had originally taken up swimming on doctor's orders. When he became Tarzan he had already made a brief appearance in movies as Adam, standing on tope of the world, naked except for a scanty fig leaf. This fleeting moment gave Weissmuller off-screen problems, because the year before he had signed a five-year contract with BVD Swimwear, and they disliked him featuring a fig leaf in place of their product; fortunately, they were smoothed down by a revised version showing Weissmuller in longshot, in which it was unclear what the champ was wearing.

BVD did not, however, design Weissmuller's famous loin-cloth. This celebrated garment caused many a heart to thump faster, and may have helped the lady journalist in *Photoplay* towards these heated conclusions: 'There is no doubt that Johnny Weissmuller possesses all the attributes both physical and mental, for the complete realisation of this son of the jungle role, with his flowing hair, his cat-like walk, and his virtuosity on the water, you can hardly ask for anything more in the way of perfection. But the most vital statistic of all is the fact that the lad who had never been in a picture before, who had been in swimming all his life, and frankly admits he can't act, is the top-notch heart flutterer of the year.' In time Weissmuller's studio image was expanded, and his word power contracted. His scriptwriters, among them Ivor Novello, shrank the ex-English lord's language down to the notorious Tarzan-Jane exchanges. The role of Jane was first played by the lovely Maureen O'Sullivan, beautifully turned out in bra and leather flaps.

In the post-war years the Tarzan recipe has continued to be successful despite more general changes in public taste which might have put that kind of outdoor male virility out of business. Weissmuller himself made a few more Tarzan movies then, replaced in the role by Lex Barker, he moved from MGM to Columbia and became Jungle Jim, on a lower budget, until 1954.

Also in the '50s, mogul Joseph Levine gave an unexpected lift to the jaded heroes of history when he put the vast weight of his publicity machine behind European-made spectaculars featuring Steve Reeves, an American actor and former Mr World and Mr Universe. Reeves's muscle-man adventures had titles like *Hercules* (1957), *Hercules Unchained* (1958), *Goliath and the Barbarians* and (spare a sentimental tear) *The Thief of Baghdad*.

Left The Rough and the Smooth: above, the hero of *The Last of the Czars* (1928) helps himself simultaneously to vodka and a peasant. Below are Johnny Weissmuller and Maureen O'Sullivan, peaceful in *Tarzan and His Mate* (1934).

A British company, Hammer Films, has ventured successfully out of doors in search of erotic possibilities. Their most successful line to date has been in Horror films (discussed in Chapter 5), but since 1965 they have also made a name for themselves in what might be called the Great Outdoors of Yesteryear. There were hints of this new direction in *She* (1965) which had Ursula Andress as the beautiful 2,000-year-old queen of a secret tribe, busy luring a young man into her valley(!) because she sees him as the reincarnation of a lover whom she had jealously murdered many years before. They bathe in the eternal flame of youth with tough results for both – though not for Hammer, who came up with a sequel, *The Vengeance of She* (1968), featuring the Czech actress Olinka Berova.

Perhaps Hammer's most famous body beautiful appeared in the company's 100th film, *One Million Years BC* (1966): Raquel Welch starred as a member of the Shell people, who chooses as a mate one of the Rock men. In the course of the action she is dropped in the sea by a pterodactyl, thereby giving her animal skins a titillating wet look. Another movie in the same line was *The Viking Queen* (1967) which contrived opportunities for open-air flagellation: a determined woman, played by an actress with the mysterious name of Carita, defeats a tyrannical Roman soldier after he has publicly flogged her naked back.

Further outdoor studies of the past, featuring primitive bikinis with the occasional monokini interspersed, have included Martine Beswick dancing in the gloaming at an outdoor feast in *Slave Girls* (1968, entitled *Prehistoric Women* in the USA); Julie Ege and Marcia Fox in *Creatures the World Forgot* (1971), and the highly publicized Victoria Vetri in *When Dinosaurs Ruled the Earth* (1970). Miss Vetri gallantly took off all her clothes except her home-made shoes to make love to Robin Hawdon in a cave; but despite this and sexy fights with giant red ants, an enormous phallic snake and a man-eating cactus, Miss Vetri never quite reached the stardom achieved by some of her blonde colleagues.

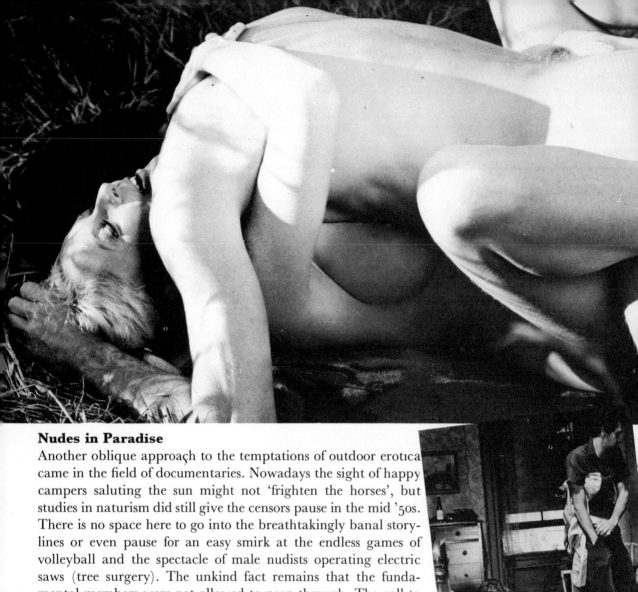

Nudes in Paradise

Another oblique approach to the temptations of outdoor erotica came in the field of documentaries. Nowadays the sight of happy campers saluting the sun might not 'frighten the horses', but studies in naturism did still give the censors pause in the mid '50s. There is no space here to go into the breathtakingly banal story-lines or even pause for an easy smirk at the endless games of volleyball and the spectacle of male nudists operating electric saws (tree surgery). The unkind fact remains that the funda-mental members were not allowed to peep through. The call to 'take off your clothes and live' meant – on celluloid anyway – shielding the pubic areas behind newspapers, deck chairs, etc. (for opening scenes, briefcases were often used to fulfil the same purpose).

By 1957, however, the New York Court of Appeals had lifted a ban on the grounds that nudity by itself was not 'sufficiently obscene to meet new standards'. In Britain there were home-spun movies like *Nudist Paradise,* which included a joyful moment as the cast play statues. *Sunswept,* on the other hand, went further, literally. A group of young men and girls travel in a yacht along the Mediterranean, visiting naturist reserves and other un-populated places. 'They were seen naked not only on land but also on the yacht,' explained John Trevelyan, the British censor. This took the film out of the category of naturist documentary. In so doing, it broke British 'Code' regulations, but eventually won distribution.

All manner of cynical excuses for showing 'sexual parts' on the screen have been offered to defend a long line of 'ethnic' studies.

Above left Joy on the grass in a US nudie that gave a new slant to an old title – *The Mark of Zorro*.
Left A bedroom scene from *Valley of the Dolls* (1967), the film that inspired Russ Meyer to go one better in 1970 with *Beyond the V of the D*.
Top A new deal for mesh-stocking fans in the French production *Filles du Soleil*.
Above Hammock owner seeks lady companion with similar interests; from *Time in the Sun* (1939), a documentary pieced together from the Russian director Eisenstein's unfinished study, *Que Viva Mexico!*
Below Kris Kristofferson goes to ground with Isela Vega in *Bring Me the Head of Alfredo Garcia* (1974).

By tradition, 'natives' could be nude and not rude (though one might have to do some delicate cutting over their circumcision rites). As such they were declared 'morally unobjectionable to adults' in the USA; but, in feature films, bare-breasted native girls had to wait until 1966 and George Roy Hill's *Hawaii*.

If movies in the naturist and 'ethnic' categories were occasionally evasive about their erotic intentions, the purpose of the 'nudies', a new genre which appeared from the late '50s onwards, was all too clear. These films are *not*, let it be said, old-style porno films with the emphasis on unrelenting sex action, and they are *not* new-style 'porno chic' on the lines of those torrid vehicles starring Linda Lovelace and her followers. They *are* (just) storyline features, and they *do* usually take place in the Great Outdoors.

Russ Meyer, an American director, will probably be best remembered as Mr Nudie. He filmed his breakthrough movie, *The Immoral Mr Teas*, in 1964. By 1974 he had moved from open-air stag operettas into the large-scale zappy absurdity of *Beyond The Valley of the Dolls*. In between he made movies such as *Vixen* (1968), shot on location in Humboldt County, California for the remarkably low price of $70,000. The rules of a 'dramatic nudie' are sex, violence and a hint of perversion, but no genitals. In *Vixen*, Tom Palmer runs a country lodge and an air charter service which he tends to operate in the nude. His oversexed, equally nude wife, the Vixen, takes advantage of his bush-piloting to make it with a Canadian Mounted Policeman; she then slips under a certain Dave King who has hired Tom's plane for a fishing trip; her own brother; Dave King's wife, and her brother's nude Negro friend. So the time passes, in a whirl of frolicking pulchritude (forest clearings are a favourite location), the whole package rounded off with a lecture on Negro equality delivered aboard a hijacked aircraft bound for Cuba.

Another American director, Paul Mart, first established himself with such titles as *Beauty and the Body* and *Sinderella and the Golden Bra*. He then moved on to make *Wild Gypsies*, which was set in a rather beautiful country location. Not so lyrical, however, were the instances of theft, drunkenness, semi-rape and murder enumerated in the plot. The story tells how Anton, a rough and frequently nude gypsy, has been drummed out of his caravan but returns under cover of darkness to have intercourse with his mistress. His passion spent, he proceeds to stab her in the navel. The girl's family are upset and plan revenge, to be executed when they are not too occupied with their own bouts of seduction, theft and fortune-telling. But the girl's brother, Juan, then dreams up a master plan which involves not only a nude appearance from himself but also requires him to snatch a white, non-gypsy girl as bait for Anton. There is just enough time to have a trial work-out, in a straw-lined barn, on the girl. All proves satisfactory. Anton then falls into Juan's trap and is killed. Finally, the avenging Juan overcomes his racial prejudice and marries his bait.

Outdoor Highlights

In recent years, what contributions has the more serious side of the movie industry made to the erotic myths of the Great Outdoors? Certainly, there has been no shortage of visual statements, some of them unforgettably attractive.

Jean Renoir, probably France's greatest director, produced in *Déjeuner sur l'Herbe* (1959) a ravishing atmosphere of light and landscape which, one might suppose, he had inherited from his painter father. Catherine Rouvel is darkly beautiful bathing naked to the waist in the river; and in the love scene Renoir focuses with superb skill on the *minutiae* of nature, on strands of grass, an insect crawling along, a stream flowing over stones.

Also in the '50s the US Beat Generation rediscovered the wide-open spaces of their native land, under the initial guidance of the novelist Jack Kerouac; later came the Flower People and the Love Generation, the themes of their philosophy beginning to emerge in cult movies such as *Easy Rider* (1970) and amid the churning rhythms and naked torsos filmed during the three famous days of *Woodstock* (1970). Movies of violence took easily to the open air: there was, for example, the aggressive wanderlust of *Bonnie and Clyde* (1967), which launched the fabulous Faye Dunaway *and* said a few things about the sexuality of spurting ketchup, used prolifically in the shoot-out scenes.

Perhaps, however, we may close this look at some sixty years of sensuality in the Great Outdoors with a gentler, yet highly potent image from Antonioni's *Zabriskie Point* (1969), the great Italian director's American feature movie – made at the time of his first visit to America – in which he showed a kind of desert love far removed from that of *The Sheik*. In this scene a host of young people copulate slowly on the dusty slopes of Death Valley, their grey, matt, bare limbs more erotically expressive in their silent, balletic flow than the automated climaxes of a hundred more overtly salacious films.

Top Celebration in Death Valley: couples mysteriously multiply and make love in Antonioni's *Zabriskie Point* (1969).
Above Sponging down during the three days of pop at *Woodstock* (1970).

Right Laya Raki, extravagantly costumed in *Die Teufelstänzerin* ('The Devil's Dancer').

DRESS AND UNDRESS

In 1963, Charles Boultenhouse, the Underground critic and film-maker, was boldly if inaccurately forecasting that 'Hollywood is the tease of all time. See how its seething teenage adorers long for the corny fantasy to turn into pornography. Reflect that it never will. No ritual orgy will be set off by a modern King and Queen of the May. The gods of the teenagers will not strip and copulate. Thus the only thing that could save the Pop art of Hollywood is precisely what will not occur.' Well, it's easy to be wrong. Or was he being ironic? It seems unlikely.

In the infant years of the movie industry, the first Queens of the May were Italian stars such as Francesca Bertini, Pina Manichelli, Maria Jacobini and Tina di Lorenzo. This was before World War I and their erotic muse was firmly chained. They were dressed not undressed, but they still worked in a heady atmosphere of plush curtains to cling to, if the brilliantined hero was not on hand, champagne to drink, death to contemplate, eulogies to bathe in, and studio power to distribute – an actor or technician's fate decided by the flicker of an eyelash.

Below Theda Bara, snaky as *Cleopatra* (1917).
Far right The stripping gets under way in this Italian version of *Quo Vadis* (1929).

When war came, Italy's pioneering efforts were quickly surpassed by the new American Dream Machine now churning away energetically in the uninterrupted Californian sun, the latter so essential to the early unsophisticated cameras. There the first-generation moguls were already handling movies like any other big-business commodity. They knew the value of films as entertainment for the huge immigrant population, escaping from their poverty and wrestling with the English language. Besides, Carl Laemmle of Universal Pictures had already set an American precedent for creating stars, with Florence Lawrence in 1910. She made the first 'personal appearance', and endured the first fake announcement of her death.

Next came William Fox with Theda Bara. She was the first really big-time star, her large, staring eyes and knowing mouth perpetuated in stills from films that have been forgotten. The name of this extraordinary creature, put about as an anagram of 'Death Arab', was really Theodosia Goodman, and she was the daughter of a Cincinatti tailor. Her body was little short of maternal, and her erotic appeal was strictly studio-made. If she later felt trapped inside her 'vampish' roles, it was not before they had made her a fortune, her fee rising from $75 a week to $4,000. Her breakthrough movie, *A Fool There Was* (1916), was based on a Broadway hit play which in turn had been inspired by Rudyard Kipling's poem 'The Vampire'. Out of his doggerel there emerged the plot of a wealthy and distinguished American abandoning money, family and eventually his own life for Bara.

A fool there was and he made his prayer
(Even as you and I!)
To a rag and a bone and a hank of hair
(We called her the woman who did not care)
But the fool he called her his lady fair –
(Even as you and I!)

The Bara myth was essentially a costume drama, heavily boosted by allusions to her mysterious 'oriental' background. Appropriately, her accoutrements included the now-notorious snake swirls curling round her breasts; while, as Alexander Walker noted, 'bead whorls appliqued on her hip bone by gum arabic looked like some satyr's erotic doodling'; there were, too, hints of perversion in her heavy jewellery, worn pressed to her naked flesh. In her behaviour she destroyed her men by direct methods, e.g. by breaking into his mansion to kiss him full on the mouth and foil the wife's forgiving embrace; and by slinking downstairs in a muslin nightie, her long hair spilling over her bare shoulders, in time to deflect a happy reunion with his little daughter. Theda Bara projected a bizarre image for her day – a fantasy vampire on the loose in Hollywood while at the same time millions of men were spilling their blood in European trenches. In its effect, though, the image was modern: in keeping with the spirit of the post-1918 world, she put 'unmarried' sex on celluloid and firmly suggested to twentieth-century women that sex was also something they might actually enjoy.

Ladies of Luxury

It was important to early Hollywood to impress its audiences with visions of luxury, not least in domestic settings that people could relate to. De Mille exemplified this in *Male and Female* (1919) with Gloria Swanson as his star. Henceforth scenes were played not just in drawing rooms but in bedrooms and bathrooms as well. The possibilities for dress and undress were miraculously multiplied.

This was the cue for actresses to become almost smothered in their own wardrobes. Joan Crawford, one of the most durable, made her début in a movie called, appropriately, *Pretty Lady* (1925). Erotic glamour was now identified with the gown, and George Hurrell, a famous Hollywood studio photographer recalled: 'Crawford would spend the whole day changing, maybe twenty different gowns, hairdos, make-up . . . she used to love getting into those forceful poses'. Betty Blythe is perhaps chiefly remembered for the erotic transparency of a single gown worn in *Queen of Sheba* (1921). But at her screen test her problem was one of dress not undress: she was asked to choose one from the thirty-six gowns called for by the part. She later said, 'I chose one with a great peacock. I'm mad for peacocks; later we had twenty-two of them on our ranch in the country. When you walked in this costume, which had pearls to the knees, the legs would come out. When you stood still, there was that glorious peacock right across the body. "Oh," I said, "the peacock – that's my deal." '

It was a basic rule of Hollywood's golden years that the stars did not strip off on film – the starlets of the chorus could do that. But their clothed eroticism was worked out in a series of finely manufactured images, of vamps and *femmes fatales* and 'It girls' and 'Bitch goddesses' and 'Ping girls' and, later, 'Sweater girls'.

Above right The sex-appeal of Joan Crawford, in *Our Blushing Brides* (1930).
Below Gloria Swanson prepares for her bath in *Male and Female* (1919).
Right Betty Blythe, flimsily draped in *Queen of Sheba* (1921).
Far right Dietrich, a German tigress.

There was even a 'genuine' Oriental girl (as opposed to Bara, who was 'manufactured'). This was Anna May Wong, one of the most photographed actresses of the 1930s: the movie *Daughter of the Dragon* had nothing to do with the art of kung-fu, but was a 1931 production featuring Miss Wong *dressed* to kill.

The Superstars naturally had Superstar costumes and publicity to extol their sexuality. This pattern was varied only by the great Garbo, who was publicized for not wanting publicity. Give or take a few hats, or the exotic costume she wore for *Mata Hari* (1932), Garbo's most compelling 'dress' was supplied by the lighting skills of the cameraman who captured her fascinating allure in nineteen out of her twenty-four pictures for MGM. The cameraman was William Daniels. On one occasion he even inserted a tiny light bulb in the tip of John Gilbert's cigarette to illuminate, in the softest way, the lovers in *Flesh and the Devil* (1927). Otherwise, Garbo's appeal stemmed from her marvellous acting and her star temperament – a flurry of kisses here, a passionate, dominant grip there; 'Garbo laughs', said the posters, 'Garbo vants to be alone', said the newspapers, abject before the melancholic Swede.

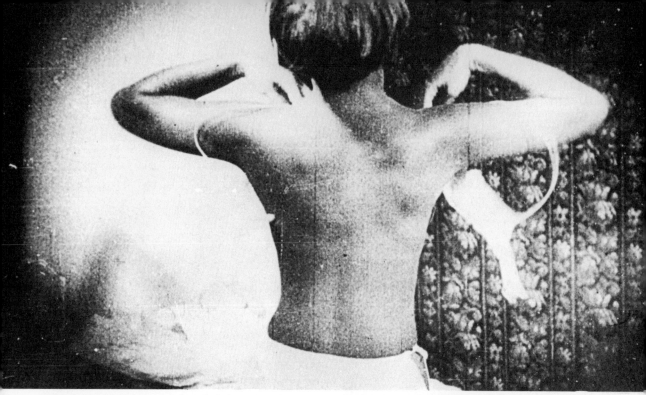

America's other celebrated import, Marlene Dietrich, had memorable outfits to complement her long stares, stunning legs and bony bisexual manner. In 1935, *Variety* said of Marlene in *The Devil is a Woman*: 'With fringe, lace, sequins, carnations, chenille, nets, embroideries and shawls, Miss Dietrich is hung, wrapped, draped, swathed and festooned. Miss Dietrich emerges . . . as a glorious achievement, a supreme consolidation of the sartorial, make-up and photographic arts.' And this is the lady who could excite an audience merely by crossing her legs, and whose androgynous impact was at its most erotic when she wore masculine clothes. Her 'Zvengali' director, von Sternberg, was contemptuous when she stripped to pose for a naked statue in a film he didn't direct – *Song of Songs* (1934).

A key figure of the '30s was Jean Harlow. Of her Parker Tyler wrote in *Sex, Psyche, Etcetera in the Film* that she 'created a totally new standard for sex goddesses. Jean was a sacred-whore type whose unabashed vulgarity (even as West's) was integral with the spell she cast.' Her flinty toughness, platinum blondness and comedy prowess were ideally suited to screen partnership with Clark Gable, notably in *Red Dust* (1932) and *China Seas* (1935). In the latter a typhoon soaks her satin gown to arousing effect. In general though, her clothes tended to cling anyway, wet or dry, and were low-cut and backless. That she had a special way with clothes was early emphasized by her much-vaunted line 'Excuse me while I slip into something more comfortable', said to hero Ben Lyon in her début in *Hell's Angels* (1930). Not a little of her erogenous credit was centred on her breasts, a department she is said to have reinstated after the leggy era of the '20s. Her statistic in that zone was not outstanding (34, as in 34-24-35), but must have seemed more so at the time.

Top Dressing or undressing? The puzzle is supplied by an unknown movie from post-revolutionary Russia, c. 1928.
Above Heart-throb Richard Barthelmess and showgirl companion in *The Noose* (1928).
Right Jean Harlow with Ben Lyon in *Hell's Angels* (1930). Harlow, who customarily helped her nipples along with ice cubes before a Press conference, also got full production value out of her fine shoulder blades, her iridescent blonde hair and her white skin, and further compounded these attractions by leading a sensational private life.

The Bosom Cult

World War II produced Hollywood sacrifices both on and off the screen. In a 1940 issue of *Silver Screen* there is an account of Joan Bennett giving blood. 'It's only natural that Joan Bennett would do something gallant, and not realize it was gallant and when asked be reluctant to talk about it . . . It will be injected, alive and lifegiving into a wounded soldier or some shattered civilian who gets in war's way.' Soldiers themselves were inclined to treat the business of war with less reverence. In *So Proudly we Hail* (1943), made in honour of the nurses who served heroically in Bataan and Corregidor, Veronica Lake, realizing at the climax that there is no hope left (the Japs are closing in) slips a live grenade into her blouse. She advances on the enemy, blowing them and herself to bits. 'I know which part I want,' shouted the GIs in the audience.

Appreciating which parts people wanted, and then supplying the goods, was of course fundamental to Hollywood knowhow. This was never clearer than in the pin-up period of the war, when low-cut dresses threw breasts into high relief, and Betty Grable's legs 'took off' by themselves, a thrill to her public and to her insurance company (they were covered for more than Fred Astaire's). In her own sweet way Miss Grable never put a thigh wrong, except in *The Shocking Miss Pilgrim* (1947) where she was dressed in Puritan clothes down to the ground. Protests from 100,000 fans ensured that her next movie was clearly labelled – *Mother Wore Tights*. In the beginning, though, her 'million dollar legs' arose out of a studio publicity stunt. Miss Grable later said in an interview: 'When I was seventeen or eighteen the studio got a new publicity man who wanted to impress them. He decided to get something splashy going and just happened to choose me. It was all fixed. He told me, "We'll run competitions and say you have the best legs". So their phoney contest took place and I was given the cup. But once they'd taken the pictures they took the cup back. Then they had my legs sculptured, but all I wanted was the cup!' All the same, the Grable legs *were* rather erotic.

Previous pages Two Mata Haris work their magic: on the left Jeanne Moreau plays the sexy agent in a 1965 version. On the right is Greta Garbo in 1931, less naked but no less fascinating.

Perhaps the best example of erotic expectations being aroused by a publicity machine is that of the protracted affair of Howard Hughes and *The Outlaw*, *circa* 1943–46. Hughes's flair for self-advertisement then was as good as it is for seclusion now. He took on Breen's office and the MPPA Code and he eventually won his tussle for the anatomy of Jane Russell – though he lost another fight over the line 'tit for tat', one of the best puns in the script. More importantly, his campaign acted as an overture for the bosom cult which has gone on in America ever since.

Undoubtedly, the focus of *The Outlaw* was fixed on Jane Russell's breasts: Hughes, an ex-aircraft engineer, himself designed her cantilevered bra and wrote obsessional memos about this section of her wardrobe. Example: 'The fit of the dress around her breasts is not good and gives the impression, God forbid, that her breasts are padded or artificial. They just don't

Left Betty Grable in 1942, amiably displaying the legs that helped to win the war.
Below Jane Russell in *The Outlaw* (1943). The publicity for this Howard Hughes venture upset the censors just as much as the film itself. 'How would you like to tussle with Russell?' trumpeted the slogan-writers, and 'What are Two Great Reasons for Jane Russell's Rise to Stardom?'
Below left A balcony view of Jayne Mansfield.

appear to be in natural contour. It looks as if she's wearing a brassiere of some very stiff material which does not take the contour of her breasts. Particularly around the nipple, it looks as though some kind of stiff material underneath the dress is forming an artificial and unnatural contour.' And on and on. Murray Schumach wrote in *The Face on the Cutting Room Floor*: 'Hughes was a great student of the obvious . . . He had her bend over Billy and had the camera peering down to her navel. He claimed this shot had never been done before. He was right. No one else in Hollywood would have dared try it.' It was later parodied in *The Carpetbaggers* (1963).

The cult spread via the sweaters of Lana Turner and the more lavishly displayed talents of lesser actresses like Jayne Mansfield, June Wilkinson and Mamie Van Doren. It was helped by the 'animal' eroticism as well as the cleavage of Ava Gardner, and by Jennifer Jones wearing Jane Russell shirts for *Duel in the Sun* (1946). It was helped by Howard Hughes inviting to America an Italian ex-fortune teller's assistant, Gina Lollobrigida: such was her universal appeal after appearances in movies like *Bread, Love and Dreams* (1953) that French bra ads began referring to *Les Lollos*. The cult was also helped by the dances of the red-haired wildcat, Rita Hayworth, and her fabulous wardrobe (discussed later in this chapter). It was thinly helped by Sabrina from Britain. Above all it was helped by the incomparable Marilyn Monroe.

The tiniest paragraph about her has to begin with a statement on her tragic vulnerability and broken-home background. OK, I begin with a statement about . . . But for this brief survey we have to concentrate on her appearance, and on the fact that with her clothes on she could still be thought too sexy (attempts were even made to tone down her famous bustline with strings of beads). Her naked calendar picture 'Golden Dreams', in addition to becoming Number One Cliché, proved she was a perfect woman in terms of her body; but the image she projected to the camera was introspective and complex (though she knew how to make perfect love to it). I have seen it argued that while sexy in

THE AMBIGUOUS MISS MONROE

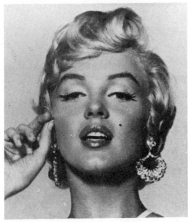

Determined to share her body with the world, Marilyn Monroe nevertheless pursued a complex and tortuous path, which eventually led to her early death – and to a place high on the list of screen immortals.
Left Cosmetically perfect but somehow resistible . . . in *How to Marry a Millionaire* (1953). Perhaps she was trying too hard.
Below At her joyous best in one of the many comedy situations in *The Seven Year Itch* (1955), in which her bubbling freshness was a perfect counterpoint to the marriage-scarred views of the Tom Ewell character.
Right In *Niagara* (1952), she takes her man with that air of cool desperation that has bemused critics ever since.

her movies she was never erotic – or at least not allowed to be due to the sensibilities of the times. To my mind she is most things to most men . . . the girl who hated her orphan clothes and dreamed of being naked in church; the girl who not only took lessons from the Actors' Studio later on in her career, but from the outset studied bone structure from medical text books to help her devise provocative poses. She was, in short, determined to share her body with the world.

She arrived in *Niagara* (1952) via *The Asphalt Jungle* (1950) and *All About Eve* (1950). Her wiggle walk in *Niagara*, one of the longest in screen history, combined with her silhouette in the shower and her notorious red dress to make her a star. In *The Seven Year Itch* (1955) she was seen to be more than good at comedy, lying in a bubble bath and wearing another dress that was caught in a blast of air from a subway grating and blew above her head, revealing the panties which at home she kookily kept in an ice-box. That was Marilyn Monroe at her best, the marvellous but fearful blonde with the rinky-dink voice who, among her many ghastly delusions, was suspicious of underwear, afraid that it would dull her skin.

Right Hollywood flirts with nudity: Maureen O'Hara as *Lady Godiva* (1955). **Left** Raquel Welch, covered up by Jim Brown in *100 Rifles* (1968). **Below left and bottom** Shower scenes in *Sweet Body of Deborah* (1972), left, and *Goodbye Columbus* (1969).

The Undress Years

Undress, such a feature of the European cinema, developed very gingerly in the USA even if it is now hard to spot a young star who 'keeps them on' when an erotic scene is somewhere round the corner. Raquel Welch is a famous exception, having made either a sincere wish or a successful gimmick out of guarding 'those four square inches' of privacy.

The year 1960 was a slow turning point for the USA. Janet Leigh, murdered in her shower in a highly erotic sequence in Hitchcock's *Psycho*, was doubly daring, showing more skin than most Hollywood actresses while also allowing herself, the female star, to be killed off in the middle of a picture. In 1961, Natalie Wood in Elia Kazan's *Splendour in the Grass* allegedly jumped naked out of her bath and ran nude down a corridor. The scene was cut from the released version. For *The Carpetbaggers* (1963) there were naked screen tests, while in the film itself Caroll Baker, who in her career has been a useful exposure barometer, revealed a fine back line, from scapula to coccyx, to add to her celebrated thumb suck in *Babydoll* (1956). A decade later, in *The Sweet Body of Deborah* (1972), she was erotically naked in a shower, passionately entwined with her husband in the story, Jean Sorel. Not that she was first in the race for an erotic shower scene: she had been pre-empted there by Ali Magraw and Richard Benjamin in *Goodbye Columbus* (1969).

An interesting test case came in the mid '60s. In *The Pawn-broker* (1965), the coloured girlfriend of the pawnbroker's assistant (Thelma Oliver playing that character most beloved of movie-makers, the good-hearted tart) takes off her dress in the shop, offering her naked breasts to the bitter pawnbroker (Rod Steiger) not out of old commercial habit – 'I'll do things you never dreamed of, pawnbroker' – but, ironically, because she wants the money to prevent her boyfriend (called Jesus) from falling in with a gang's plan to rob the shop. It was a very short scene, intercut with shots revealing the pawnbroker's thoughts, preoccupied with the past and his wife's humiliation in a Nazi camp brothel. On this occasion the MPPA split with the Catholic Legion of Decency, and passed the picture. By the end of the following year the Code had been radically revised, in time to operate its new SMA rating (Suggested for Mature Audiences) for *Who's Afraid of Virginia Woolf* (1967) – and to watch almost all the other taboos come tumbling after.

Nudity has been a primary taboo for so long that even in the freer post-pubic climate of the '70s, the audience still tends to get some sort of erotic *frisson* from watching a couple, whether they are in the higher metaphysical state called love or merely in the physical state called undressed. That said, it is what two such bodies may register, either in their fusion or in the signals they exchange, that makes up the final texture of erotica. Moreover, they don't have to be naked to transmit an erotic effect. In European movies this is borne out by the work of two major directors, Ingmar Bergman and Michelangelo Antonioni.

A parallel offered between the two directors, other than their intellectualism, has been that of a shared sense of 'journeying', Antonioni's being the more haphazard. It is also customary to spotlight Bergman's involvement with the bizarre and his bleakly erotic examination of physical and psychological abnormalities. He nevertheless also deals in more elegant images, with candlelight and cut glass and formal dining tables, focusing at some precisely calculated moment on the poised gesture of a hand, the intimacy of a whisper, the compelling eyes of his extraordinary actresses. These are the women who have passed the torch from one to another over twenty years, Mai-Britt Nilsson to Harriet Andersson and Eva Dahlbeck, to Bibi Andersson to Ingrid Thulin to Liv Ullmann.

Part of Bergman's appeal lies in his ability to write good parts for women and in his ability to work with them. Liv Ullmann has said in an interview: 'I think he finds it easier to work with actresses because they are far less afraid of undressing – not their bodies but their minds.' When the stripping-away process terminates, as it often does, in violence, the erotic shock can be all the stronger because of the quieter exchanges that have gone before. In *Persona* (1965) Alma (Bibi Andersson) waits for Elizabeth (Liv Ullmann) to cut her foot on a piece of glass; in *The Silence* (1963) a woman in bed masturbates herself to climax. Also in *Persona*, in an exceptionally well-written monologue, Alma talks to Elizabeth of experiences long buried away, of a passionate sexual encounter with a young boy on a beach; the scene demonstrates the erotic power of words, spoken, Bergman later said admiringly, 'in a voice which carries a tone of shameful lust, and I've no idea where she got it from'. The overall message, argues Robin Wood in his study of Bergman, is more life-enhancing than is often supposed. 'The characteristic movement of an Antonioni film is towards a defeat that has something in it of self-indulgence, so little energy is summoned up to combat it; that of a Bergman film is a dynamic drive from sickness and imprisonment towards a health and freedom not necessarily reached but passionately sought.'

Antonioni, by contrast, tends to 'drift', mainly in a quiescent landscape, his actions consisting of character studies of bored upper-class people that are short on incident and involve lovers who are short on physical contact. In *Eclipse* (1962), a wistful pursuit of consummation ends in the anti-climax of an unkept rendezvous; in *The Red Desert* (1964) a neurotic heroine lies on her bed alone, her varying moods expressed in different colours. As Parker Tyler explains, Antonioni's films 'show simple eroticism as base, as in the incidental seduction of the young painter in *L'Avventura*, or psychopathic, as in the hospital incident in *La Notte*. In the world of sane and serious women, says Antonioni, making physical contact is a great problem.'

This oblique approach to eroticism is unusual among European film-makers, especially once television and taboo-breaking had begun to revolutionize standards and tastes. The Scandinavians

Top One of the great Bergman stars, Ingrid Thulin, here shares her bed with Dirk Bogarde in *The Damned* (1969).
Above More than one reason for doing things by halves: Yugoslav actress Sylva Koscina in *Alone with a Crime* (1972).
Right Essy Persson, leading attraction in the Danish film *I, a Woman* (1965) which grossed more than $1 million in the USA.

led the advance. They had Essy Persson for the open market and Marie Liljedahl for the closed. The most successful Scandinavian film in the USA (*I a Woman*, Denmark, 1965) starred Essy Persson as a highly undressed nymphomaniac and grossed over $1 million for its distributor, Radley Metzger. She went on to play exciting outdoor games with Anna Gael in *Thérèse and Isabelle* (1969). The Swedes, lyrical for so long in the Great Outdoors, also became lyrical in bed. For an example we might take the happy nude lovers in *Dear John* (1964), directed by Lars Magnus Lindgren, which featured Jarl Kulle as a middle-aged man, and Christina Schollin as a young 'pick-up' waitress.

As the 1960s progressed, Italy made its spaghetti cowboy films and period neo-epics; France wondered who could succeed Brigitte Bardot; Germany plodded on with sex education, and Britain slowly capitalized on the mental exposures of *Room at the Top* (1959), and the notion expressed by a newly deflowered virgin that 'sex is super'. There was, too, Julie Christie. Dressed as a fashion model for most of John Schlesinger's *Darling* (1965), she eventually undressed in a studiedly unerotic way and walked through the rooms of a large Italian *palazzo*, a symbol of her own despair. The US took no chances and cut this naked backview, though in 1967 they allowed Hayley Mills's skimpy buttocks to rise modestly from the wash tub in a working-class kitchen (*The Family Way*, 1967).

The Stripgirls

Meanwhile, back at the spectacular, America was producing its final round of heroines from the ancient world, their clothing equally suited to Mount Olympus and Forest Hills. Rosanna Podesta was the 1955 *Helen of Troy*; a year earlier Lana Turner stole the costume show with *The Prodigal*, in which she embodied every pubescent lad's dream of what high priestesses were made of. More interesting still are the fiery antics of Rita Hayworth, who in a series of exotic parts managed to establish that she didn't have to take much off to enchant her audiences.

In *Salome* (1953) she went as far as the fourth veil in a twisted plotline which had her dancing to *save* the head of John the Baptist. The fourth veil was a technical advance on *Gilda* (1946), where she only peeled off a black glove, and also on *Sadie Thompson* (1954) where she did bumps and grinds and, fully clothed, sang 'Put the Blame on Mame' like the fallen angel she was supposed to be.

Above and right Dynamic wardrobe effects by Rita Hayworth, who proved in her films that you don't have to strip to be erotic.
Below Lana Turner, tops as a high priestess in *The Prodigal* (1954).

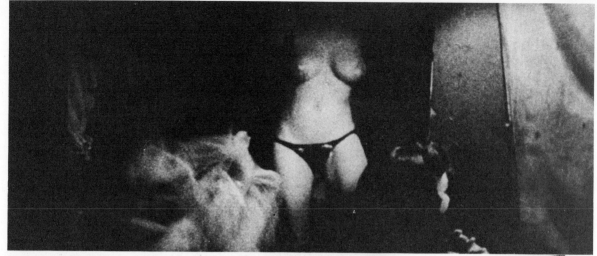

The true stripper and her imitators nevertheless play a useful role in movies. They may be found in straightforward striptease movies, or in dramas either involving exotic dancers or which are set in a night-life background; or they may appear in a strip scene injected to lend spice and vigour to the storyline surrounding it. There have been a host of these situations ever since Georges Méliès borrowed a few girls from the Folies Bergère (*circa* 1900) to embroider his 'trick photography'. Since this is one of the most logical aspects of dress and undress, we will just mention four examples. Working backwards in time, French director Claude Chabrol has a splendid prostitute dancing a Salome routine for a private client in *Nada* (1974); they are then rudely interrupted by a band of revolutionaries. In *The Spy Who Came in from the Cold* (1965) Richard Burton as the down-at-heel spy sourly watches a strip act in a Soho club; while in Joseph Strick's exposé-documentary, *The Savage Eye* (1959), a stripper reaching fake orgasm snarls 'I'd never get pregnant this way'. Finally, in *Le Destin Execrable de Guillemette Babin* (1948), a costume drama, there is an outdoor striptease by a royal lady who anachronistically reaches the climax of her act in a rather 1948-style *cache-sexe*.

Top Boobs in the gloom in *The Savage Eye* (1960). At the climax of her act the stripper snarls: 'I'd never get pregnant this way'.
Above left Leg-baring by Silvana Mangano in *Bitter Rice* (1951).
Above Great actresses also strip – at least, in France they do: Edwige Feuillère in *Sans Lendemain* (1940).
Right Nude in uniform: Charlotte Rampling, strange victim of *The Night Porter* (1974).
Overleaf In the Kingdom of Fantasy: Malcolm McDowell learns to kick the habit in *A Clockwork Orange* (1971), and girls on swings hover mysteriously in *Barbarella* (1968).
Page 100 The joys of shooting women; from *Layout for Five Models* (1974).

Below Loren strips for Mastroianni in
Yesterday, Today and Tomorrow (1963).
Bottom Cover-up on Stella Stevens – by
Dean Martin in *The Silencers* (1966).

Body Language

Also relevant to this chapter is a range of much more subtle 'uniforms' of love . . . small physical statements and signals that audiences eternally have recognized and responded to. Some of these have more to do with anatomy than costume or cosmetics, but in the fleeting world of gesture to which they belong it becomes more difficult to separate and categorize. As examples of this more muted form of erotic display, we may briefly cite the eyes of Audrey Hepburn, the highly defined eyebrows of Elizabeth Taylor, the smile of Jeanne Moreau, the teeth of x, the ears of y, the O of o, a hairstyle, a walk, a caress, a comedy secretary bending over the filing cabinet. Still with our gaze applied to the viewfinder, we find lips made not just for kissing but for pouting, or parted to reveal a moist tongue slid out in a curl of expectation; we see sexual horseplay, we see onanism, a girl plucking at her own nipples. We see the attraction of bare female arms slid round the neck of a lover's rough-knit jersey.

It was André Malraux who adapted the classics to say: 'The East has opium, the West has woman'. And today's woman has a far greater armoury of erotic effects than ever before. She has stepped away from the naive pleasantries of yesteryear: in bedroom scenes she is no longer obliged to dash from her bed in backview and quickly grab some clothes to cover herself. Today,

Top Steve McQueen in *Papillon* (1973) takes rice with one of those beautiful, trusting native girls (Ratna Assan) with which the forests of filmland are inexhaustibly populated.
Above A tolerable way to spend *Perfect Friday* (1970): Stanley Baker gazes in some disbelief at Ursula Andress.

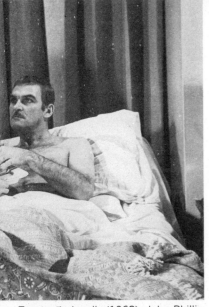

Top In *Barbarella* (1968), John Phillip Law and Anita Pallenberg make love near the mouth of a hugely suggestive tunnel, the latter big enough to have accepted penetration by Hitchcock's train at the lovers' climax in *North by Northwest*.
Inset Robert Redford in *Downhill Racer*.

more options are open to her. She may saunter, instead, naked to the window and greet the dawn (Elemental); or appear 'full frontal' in the maid's lace cap to serve her master with a cup of tea (Male Fantasy); or (Female Fantasy) she may pour it over his head. More things are now possible in the name of Eros than were once dreamed of.

As a Man Friday footnote, we might add that the world has taken a long time to prepare for Tarzan to lose his loincloth. Male stars for most of movie history, give or take a few Ramon Novarros and miscellaneous heaving chests, have flaunted their *machismo* but not their bodies. This reticence to expose has fostered a more oblique approach; applying it, stars such as Paul Newman and Robert Redford exert far more pulling power than, say, Linda Lovelace and Georgina Spelvin achieve by more explicit methods.

Blue of eye and steely of purpose, swift on the draw or the quip, suave in dress and manner, men operate according to a different set of standards. What appears different about these standards is that they were traditionally controlled, and to some extent still are, by the requirements of a certain type of fan – the middle-of-the-road *female* moviegoer. And, as we mentioned at the beginning of Chapter 1, she is inclined to judge her men more by what they *do*, or threaten to do, than by what they *show*.

Above and far right Two male idols who died young: Bruce Lee, first and greatest of the Kung fu stars, and James Dean, here in *East of Eden*.
Above right Turning to the front, Joe Dallesandro (and Sylvia Miles) in *Heat*.

Male film stars seem also to command greater loyalty than their female counterparts. Take for example the elevation into cult status of certain male stars who died young: there was Valentino, revered by women in the '20s; James Dean, revered

by young people in the '50s; and Bruce Lee, a dead warlord of the present decade.

On the undress side, things have speeded up considerably in our more liberated sexual climate. The plethora of present-day rearview nudity was prodded along by various films in the mid '60s, among them *Zorba the Greek* (1965) and *Ulysses* (1967). Also in 1965 Lars Gorling's *Guilt* caused a stir among the censors because it showed a man undressing to go to bed and in the process briefly exposing his penis. Very soon all kinds of movie frontiersmen were going to turn and face their audiences. By 1975, the guidelines on male dress had been largely erased.

This page Thighs : now the Inside Story can be told.
Right Edwardian mount.

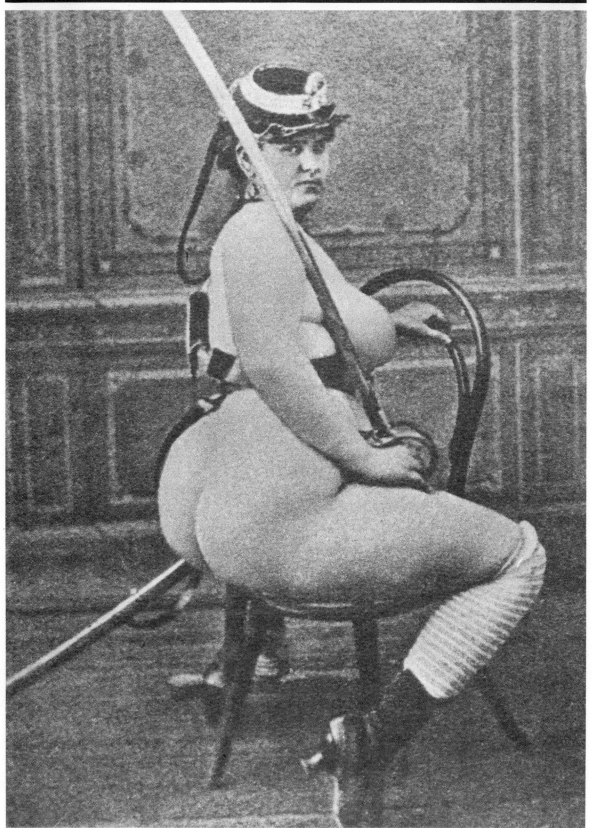

The erotic cinema uses symbols in two principal ways – to represent the human sex organs, their potency frozen in the shape of, for example, Busby Berkeley's famous bananas, or as substitutes for an erotic happening. Examples of the latter category are the tumbling waves in *From Here to Eternity* (1953), the fireworks in *To Catch a Thief* (1955), rearing stallions in *Extase* (1933) and *Not as a Stranger* (1955), and the train rushing into the tunnel in *North by Northwest* (1959). There is, too, a school of directors, the Surrealists, whose members probe symbolism in a deeper, more disturbing form. We shall tackle them towards the end of the chapter.

Just as the Victorian postcard world went in for male and female symbols, hard and soft – chimney stacks and popping champagne bottles, pigeons, hearts and figures of eight – so the movie-makers have made ample use of guns and gear-levers on the one hand, and of moonlight and water on the other. They have used them to create certain moods, and also as a means of circumventing the censor. Shades of the latter still survive, although as love-making on the screen has become more and more graphic, so the symbol as a cover-up has tended to be abandoned or turned into parody.

But there is still no shortage of material for those who seek it. In the world of symbols the ghost of Freud or Krafft-Ebing can accompany every zoom on to a mountain top or slow pan up to the sun. (I was once told an amusing story by a pretty actress of an American film producer's attempt to seduce her in his luxury apartment. All else failing, he put his faith in symbolism, rushed to his record-player and flung on 'Climb Every Mountain' from *The Sound of Music*.)

More seriously, the work of Michelangelo Antonioni offers several prime examples of symbolism in operation, and also demonstrates how powerful such symbolism can be. His film *Blow-up* (1966) tells the story of a photographer, David Hemmings, who thinks he has witnessed a murder and in a long silent sequence blows up a picture in his darkroom in search of more evidence. The film has two especially erotic moments in it. One is for real, as two young 'groupies' eagerly strip the photographer and themselves on his studio floor. The other is symbolic, as Hemmings crouches beside and over a writhing photographic model, and 'orgasmically' takes numerous shots of her. It is an immensely strong image. The girl, incidentally, was played by the extraordinary real-life model, Veruschka, who then became a film actress and something of a walking symbol herself, her body memorably painted on one occasion to transform her into a psychedelic bald-headed Salome.

In an earlier Antonioni film, *L'Avventura* (1959), a girl, Anna, goes missing and much is made of the barren volcanic island on which the search for her is made; the island becomes a symbol of the desolation felt by her friends on losing her. Before this, when Sandro, Anna and her best friend Claudia are on board their yacht, Anna makes a present to Claudia of a dress. This is seen by Parker Tyler, in *Sex, Psyche, Etcetera in the Film*, as a 'symbolic anticipation of her replacement, by Claudia, as Sandro's lover'.

Top left The stuck-on dollar girl . . . Marisa Mell arranges herself for a scene in *Danger–Diabolik*.
Above Busby Berkeley's fruity concept for the 'Brazil' number in *The Gang's All Here* (1943).
Left David Hemmings homes in with his lens on model Veruschka in *Blow Up* (1966).
Right Ewa Aulin in *Candy* (1968). Fly her.
Overleaf Now fly them.

Female clothes, especially underclothes, have a natural sexual association. In *Shoot the Pianist* (1960), Michele Mercier propositions rather sweetly with her knickers as she lurks behind a screen. More than thirty years earlier, in *The Wind* (1928), a budding passion between Lillian Gish and a pastor (Lars Hanson) is delicately emphasized by a shot of the underwear she has been washing, shown abandoned on a bush. Elsewhere in the film the wind itself is given great symbolic force, and there is even a white stallion kicking up its heels in the clouds as Gish shoots a would-be rapist. The white horse is of course a much-favoured symbol representing potency and freedom; it was perhaps used to best advantage at the close of *Viva Zapata*, made in 1952.

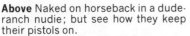

Above Naked on horseback in a dude-ranch nudie; but see how they keep their pistols on.
Right Cowpoke to girl: 'Listen, you're embarrassing my horse.'

Bring on the Horses

Horse power is a large theme on its own and we don't have to search very far to see its symbolic potential; the riding of the animal alone serves as an image of mastery – quite apart from the time spent taming it in the corral or grappling with it at the rodeo. It's Parker Tyler again who analyses the horse as a 'totem animal'. He singles out *Homestretch* as typical of a certain genre of horse-racing story in which 'the fate of the romance and the winning of the race are duly dovetailed'. 'Let us not be squeamish,' says he, 'about the horse race as a symbolic variety of the sexual act . . . the obsessional temper of racing fans and the emotional build-up to a minutes-long suspense (the race itself) accompanied by thè wildest excitement and breathlessly climaxed, are factors of racing that testify to its sexual parallel.' With all due respect, I am thankful that Mr Tyler didn't get his hands on *National Velvet* (1944), in which, you may recall, a very young Elizabeth Taylor dresses up as a male jockey, wins the Grand National, faints, falls, is found to be a girl, and so is disqualified. (The year before, by the way, she had made her début in *Lassie Come Home*, but I am leaving dogs out of it.)

Without doubt, the horse is man's second-best symbol. This is borne out on one level by a long trail of sentimental horse operas such as *My Friend Flicka* (1943) in which Roddy McDowall is the boy isolated on a farm who seeks symbolic power by befriending and mastering a mare, and then the mare's son; and on another level by the hard riding and 'good fellowship' in *Butch Cassidy and the Sundance Kid* (1971). Parker Tyler also makes mention of the movie *Indiana*, which 'portrays an adolescent romance in which the boy, by stealth, clandestinely mates two fine racehorses belonging to two different stables; not only did this incident provide, in the more obvious sense, a symbolic conjugation with the girl he loved, but also a totemic rite in which the boy could eavesdrop on the parental marriage-bed'. As for *The Outlaw*, we can apparently forget Jane Russell and her producer's devotion to the bra as 'routine innuendos', even if 'lewd and nude'. The erotic sym-

Above Robert Mitchum with gun, and bare-chested for good measure, in *His Kind of Woman* (1951).
Right Gunman with both hands full; from a Polish movie, *The Agent from HARM*.
Below Jack Nicholson as the stick-up man in *The Cry Baby Killer* (1958).

bolism is far more alarming. Billy the Kid (played by newcomer Jack Buetel) sets out to avenge the killing of his brother. A stallion which used to belong to Billy and now is technically owned by a friendly rival outlaw called 'Doc' (he calls the horse 'sweetheart') becomes a bone of contention between them. 'The stallion is an actual love-object,' says Tyler, 'a co-extended Narcissus image for each male; certain details indicate that for "Doc" the attractive boy becomes homosexually symbolic of the horse.' Howard Hughes, where are you now!

Bang! Bang!

Man's *best* symbol is his gun. Here there is no end to the illustrations, but Harry Schein said it all when he wrote *Shots in the Dark* in 1956. 'The gun of the westerns is a classic penis-symbol. In a long series of movies the weapon itself is at the center of the action. He who owns the weapon is unconquerable . . . The good men are the rightful owners, the bad ones try to steal their potency.' The weapon is 'firm and long and fired from the hip. It is very important how you get it out. Bad men get it out often but too slowly. Like Casanova they shoot in all directions without hitting anything. The hero who defends his family and his home gets his weapon out quickly. He shoots rarely but he never misses. As an upholder of society he cannot be promiscuous. There must be a result from every shot. A strong man can fire six shots without reloading.'

So, too, with non-Westerns. In crime movies there is an additional phallic attachment – the silencer. Guns no longer fire in films, they ejaculate, driving the recipient back against the car seat (*Bonnie and Clyde*, 1967), or against the wall (*The Day of the Jackal*, 1973). As if this were not enough for the male power complex, movie erotica has handled plenty of other weapons, too, from avenging swords, daggers and axes to police truncheons and the erectile fighting legs of Bruce Lee. One of the most subtle, and deadly, applications was that of the eponymous knife in Polanski's *Knife in the Water* (1961).

Colours, Shapes and Eating Habits

It is well known in the exotic dancing business that the colours and materials of stage costumes convey distinct messages of their own to the members of the audience. In an appropriate context, colours such as black, red and purple will represent unusual sex; while pastel shades will appeal to the viewer whose appetites are for gentler entanglements, e.g. with the girl-next-door, real-life maiden type. Among fabrics, leather is rough, satins and silks are sexily lush, and so on.

Statues were at one time familiar props in movies that dealt with aspects of sexuality, and they were used both *directly* and *directionally*. In James Broughton's *The Pleasure Garden* (1951), a man puts a fig-leaf over the private parts of a male statue; and in *End of Innocence* (1957) a young girl plants a surreptitious kiss on the lips of a stone angel. In the serious cinema today, such images have become largely redundant, as well as subject also to a certain amount of gleeful parody.

On the not-so-serious side, musical statues have a long history extending back to the *poses plastiques* and the *tableaux vivants* of the 19th century. In movies, they were never better used than by the superbly inventive Busby Berkeley, who fashioned his chorus girls into an astonishing range of tableaux, touched with his magical sense of the erotic; while, almost at the end of the subtlety spectrum, there has been little to compare with the high-camp symbolism of the costume that Carmen Miranda wore for 'The Lady in the Tutti Frutti Hat' in *The Gang's All Here* (1943). Such phallic fun only became more overt (apart, that is, from the real McCoy) in the gruesome masks of *A Clockwork Orange* (1973), and the plaster cast of a penis (*WR, Mysteries of the Organism*, 1971), which ostensibly gave the legitimate cinema its first male erection.

In passing, we should also mention the symbolic use of food. As a pretend-aphrodisiac it was famously exploited in Tony Richardson's *Tom Jones* (1963): the masticating molars belonged to Albert Finney and Joyce Redman as each tore at chunks of meat while ogling the future bed partner with unwavering eyes, gravy trickling pást their sensuously churning cheeks to drip, unheeded, from their chins. In contrast, food was put to more representational use in *Women in Love* (1970), a movie based on D. H. Lawrence's story. Here the erotic foreplay reaches a 'high' as Alan Bates splits and strokes a fresh fig to discuss its properties with his lady companions.

Far left The threat of the knife, in Hitchcock's *Blackmail* (1930), the first British talkie.
Above The machete is poised to strike, but she seems to be enjoying it; from an 'ethnic' movie, *Tictaban*.
Left Bony fingers dent the victim's flesh in one of the spookier images from an early Swedish venture into the supernatural, *Witchcraft through the Ages* (1919).

Witches and Vampires

Witchcraft has the advantage for the erotic movie-maker of a built-in symbolism that comes complete with naked ceremonials. In addition, it offers a convenient excuse for the showman to exhibit something marginally *risqué* in the guise of documentary truth. Sweden understood this principle very early on, and *Witchcraft through the Ages* (1919), despite its unstimulating title, produced some notable stills of pagan rituals and devil worship.

The appeal of this hammy, half-lit world has meant big business for the media: books, magazines and movies proliferate at the popular end of the market, all holding out the same enticing yet

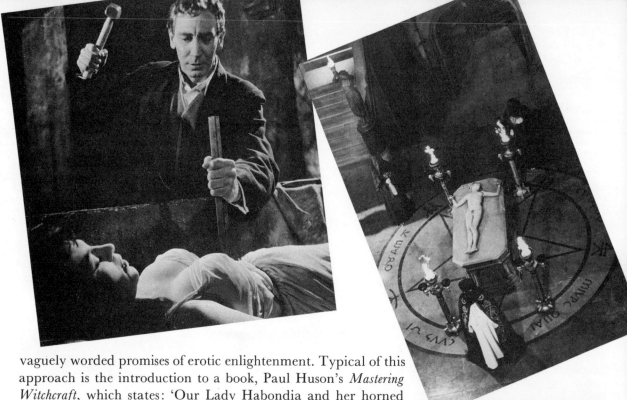

vaguely worded promises of erotic enlightenment. Typical of this approach is the introduction to a book, Paul Huson's *Mastering Witchcraft*, which states: 'Our Lady Habondia and her horned consort hold court once more. Should you wish to tread the dark path of witchcraft, the way is open to you now. Whether you believe the Christian bugaboos and fear to lose your soul, or like us, consider the gamble well spent, is up to you.'

The gamble, as far as the film companies are concerned, has been well worth while. Enter, then, the nude postulant to stand outside the magic circle, wrists bound behind her with cord, a dagger posed over her heart to symbolize the gravity of her vows. Enter high priestesses and pentacles and a thurible burning an incense of wrath and a chalice of bitter wine and a wand and a red unlit candle of bewitchment and lamps and phials of Sabbat oil and a Square of Mars and baneful herbs and graveyard dust and Dagydes. Enter a vulnerable maiden to lie even more vulnerably upon an altar.

These and related ingredients have made many a tasty dish to set before the movie public. One company that has more than dabbled in the occult is Britain's Hammer Films. They have in fact been running at top speed for nearly twenty years – winning, symbolically enough, the Queen's Award to Industry on the way. Their more recent ventures in sensational entertainment reveal, fundamentally, a two-pronged approach. They go for symbolic sex in the Great Outdoors set among dinosaurs and assorted monsters (see Chapter 3) and also for the more explicitly sexual escapades of witches and the blood-lettings of vampires. On the basis that titles sell such movies, let some Hammer titles speak for themselves: *The Bride of Dracula* (1960), *Kiss of the Vampire* (1964), *The Witches* (1966), *Dracula Has Risen from the Grave* (1968), *The Vampire Lovers* (1970), *Lust for a Vampire* (1971), and *Dracula is Dead and Well and Living in London* (1973).

Top left It's curtains for the she-vampire, extinguished by the traditional stake through the heart.
Top right The paraphernalia of devil worship, arrayed in *Twins of Evil*.
Above Peter Cushing takes the wraps off a new model in the Hammer film *Frankenstein Created Woman*.
Right Muriel Catala, provocative in *Verdict* (1974).
Overleaf, top left David Warbeck strikes again in *Sex Thief*.
Centre left Georgina Spelvin, showing off in *The Devil and Miss Jones* (1974).
Bottom left Sacheen Littlefeather is a rape victim in *Johnny Firecloud*.
Right Clint Eastwood drops his gun-belt for Jessica Walter in *Play Misty*.
Page 120 Ride on – Marie Liljedahl puts Julian Mateos through his paces in *Ann and Eve*.

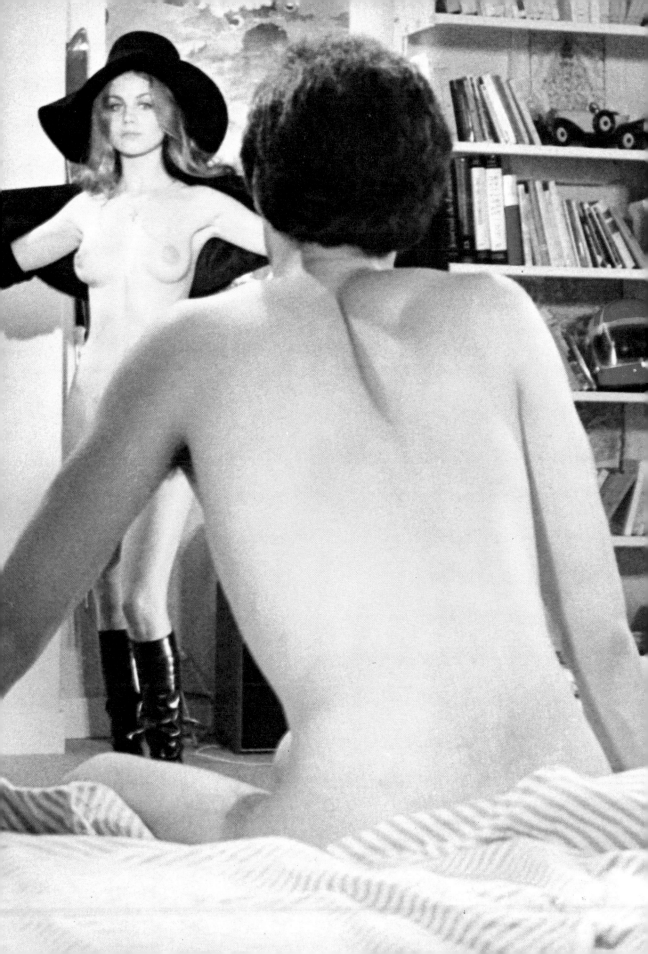

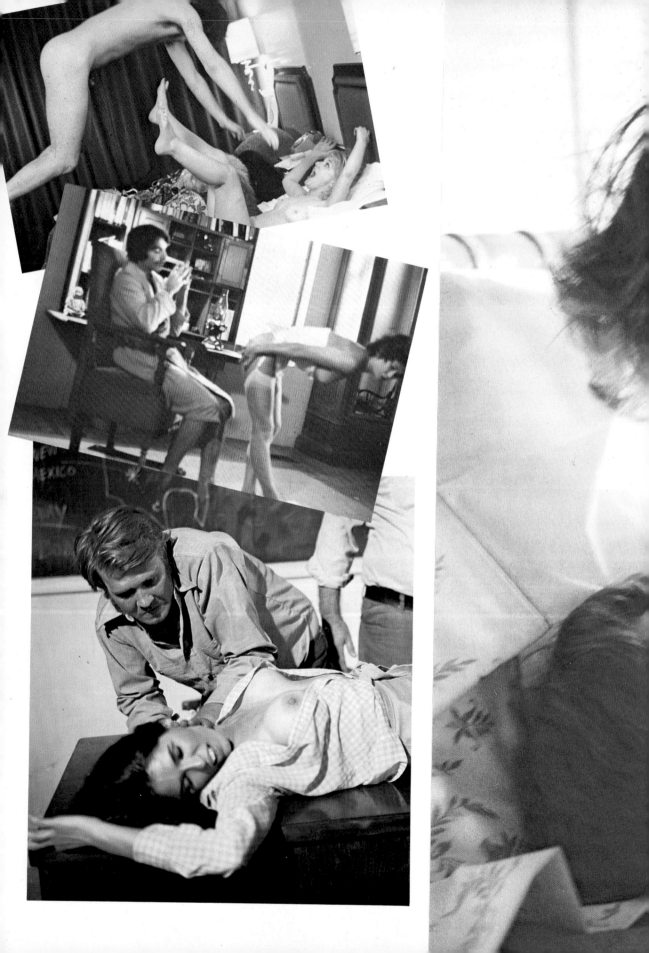

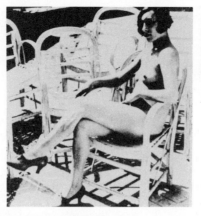
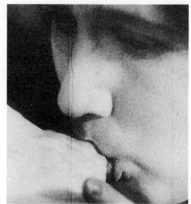

The Surrealists

The masters of experiment with sex and symbol have unquestionably belonged to that group of film-makers known as the Surrealists, the most famous single combination being that of the Spanish painter Salvador Dali and a fellow Spaniard, Luis Bunuel, considered by many to be Europe's greatest film director. Bunuel has never totally abandoned this aspect of his work in more than forty years of film-making. *Un Chien Andalou* (1928) bulges with images from the subconscious; among those most often quoted are the eye slashed with a razor and the ants' nest in the palm of a living hand. The images provide a form of erotic shock, in which hate acts as the familiar corollary of love. There is also the well-known shot of a man fondling a girl's breasts which turn into buttocks. Another Bunuel movie, *L'Age d'Or* (1930), produced such potent images as that of Christ in the guise of the Marquis de Sade, and of a woman sucking the toe of a marble statue; while Germaine Dulac's *La Coquille et Le Clergyman* (1926) used the sea shell as a symbol of a naked girl. In the 1930s in America the themes of sexual substitution and seduction by monsters were developed in the horror films of James Whale – *Frankenstein* (1931) and *Bride of Frankenstein* (1935) – and Tod Browning – *Dracula* (1930), *Mark of the Vampire* (1935) and *The Devil Doll* (1936).

Those movies were in turn a few post-Freudian steps away from the American New Wave cinema of the '40s and '50s. At that time an avant-garde group centred on directors like James Broughton, Maya Deren, Marie Mencken and the precocious Kenneth Anger made several rather obscure films, mostly on 16mm. Their symbolic content could be blindingly clear, however, as in Kenneth Anger's movie, *Fireworks*, made in 1947 when he was only seventeen. In one of the film's most memorable moments, a Roman candle sticking out of a Marine's open fly fizzes and bursts in a shower of stars.

Evidently, this branch of symbolism embraces much tougher sexual imagery than the more traditional flames in the fireplace, rain on the window pane, the slow pan up to the heavens or even horses in the sky. There is a wonderful 1924 film poster of Douglas Fairbanks Snr starring in *The Thief of Baghdad*. He rides across the heavens on a white horse, erect scimitar in hand. Today, no question, he would be on a motor bike.

Top left The quick-change artiste in Jean Vigo's *A Propos de Nice* (1930): in one frame she appears clothed, in the next naked.
Top right Love me, love my statue; from *L'Age d'Or* (1930).
Above In James Broughton's *The Pleasure Garden* (1951), John Le Mesurier nails a fig leaf on to a male statue.
Below Weals within wheels in the magic land of *Eden and After* (1970).

Above Mary Murphy falls by the wayside after a spin on Marlon Brando's bike in *The Wild One* (1954).
Below The spread hair tells its own story: Charlotte Rampling in *'Tis Pity She's a Whore*.

Eros on a Motor Bike

The sexual symbolism of machinery is a large topic for which we have only limited space. We can, however, look at the implications of one aspect – the motor bike. While we would not suggest that behind each 'rev' there lies an ejaculation, the bike's image of threatening potency is continually there for all to see and hear. Marlon Brando played the lead in *The Wild One* (1954), which was about a gang of motor-cycle hooligans who terrorize a small town. It was a vintage year for the astonishing Brando (*On the Waterfront* was also a 1954 movie) and as with several of his films there were censorship repercussions. The problem here was the nature of the violence, and Britain effectively banned the film until 1969, when it was admitted with an X certificate. (That is, it was banned except in one cinema, managed at that time by Leslie Halliwell, author of an invaluable and ever-expanding guide, *The Filmgoer's Companion*; Halliwell had managed to secure the approval of his local Watch Committee.) In the film Kathie (Mary Murphy) rides pillion behind Johnny (Brando), registering a precisely calculated mix of agony and ecstasy, and at the end of the journey she sinks to the ground and strokes the machine. It seemed stronger meat in those palmy, far-off days.

Motor bikes also starred with Elvis Presley in *Roustabout*, and with Steve McQueen, a keen rider in private life, who did his own stunt sequence for *The Great Escape* (1963); and, of course, in *Easy Rider* (1972).

The Hells Angels (alias *The Wild Angels*, 1966) may have added an extra brutality to the bike-movie scene, but for subtle erotic menace there has been little to match the outriders of death who feature in *Le Testament d'Orphée* (1960), black-goggled creatures drawn from the flaring, poetic imagination of Jean Cocteau.

The post-war cinema teems with evidence of symbols being consciously applied to express an erotic idea. The movies they appear in, and the effects they create, range from the naively comic, e.g. snorkels poking about underwater in a 1950s nudist movie, to the purposefully dramatic: Anouk Aimée, brought by Marcello Mastroianni to make love on a prostitute's bed (*La Dolce Vita*, 1959); a man strokes a cat sitting beside a girl in bed (*The Seven Deadly Sins*, 1952); *Claire's Knee* is touched, not by some casual groper but as the climactic act of will of a shy philosophical hero (1971).

In a lighter vein, we end with one of the fun lines of film history. In 1955 a Damon Runyon story was turned into the enchanting musical *Guys and Dolls*. In the film version Marlon Brando plays the crooked gambling anti-hero Sky Masterson, whose father had taught him never to take ill-considered bets or he would get 'cider in his ear'. A desperate Nathan Detroit (Frank Sinatra) bets him in a restaurant that he won't be able to take out to dinner the next girl he sees. The bet is made and Nathan points through the window – to a Salvation Army girl (Jean Simmons) shaking her tambourine on the sidewalk. 'Daddy,' sighs Sky heavily, 'I've got cider in my ear.'

TOTEM AND TABOO

It cannot be over-emphasized that in Greek mythology Eros (known to the Romans as Cupid) was the god of *love*. Consequently, what that cuddly little chap got up to, with his folds of baby flesh and his quiver filled with arrows, was not all sex. Love, to remind us of three misleading film tags, is not only 'a many splendoured thing', but 'never having to say you are sorry' (*Love Story*) and also 'a four-letter word'. It is also a glance, a nuance, a sensual suggestion. Nevertheless, we treat it here more in its four-letter capacity.

Nudity, as we have already outlined, was a basic taboo which has only reached anything approaching a general level of acceptance in recent times. There is still considerable caution over exposing male genitals, the sexual implications of even the relaxed male penis apparently being very strong.

A pretty girl undressing has a certain erotic appeal for men and women, and one doesn't have to be an obsessive voyeur or a lesbian to find it so. Not surprisingly, both situations have been exploited in movies, under such excessively simple titles as *The Voyeur* and *Women without Men*. Whether or not that girl, or girls in general, was to be allowed to show her pubic hair has been one of the great battles of the cinema. In Britain, a test case came in 1968 with a Swedish film called *Hugs and Kisses*, where the heroine (played by Agneta Ekmanner, the director's wife) looks at herself naked in a mirror. Pubic hair was seen and banned, and then deliberately shown to the Press as banned. John Trevelyan, the censor, later explained that the distributor had invited him to meet the Press and give his reasons: 'I

Previous page Sue Lyon as *Lolita* (1962), the Nabokov heroine who made nymphets fashionable.
Top Free-wheeling sex in Makavejev's taboo-busting *WR, Mysteries of the Organism* (1971). The girl is Jagoda Kaloper.

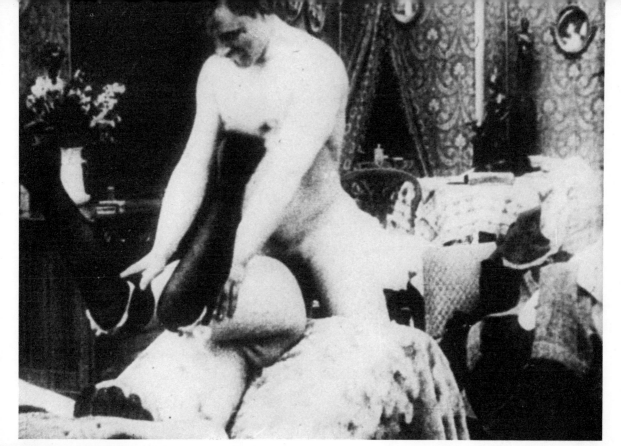

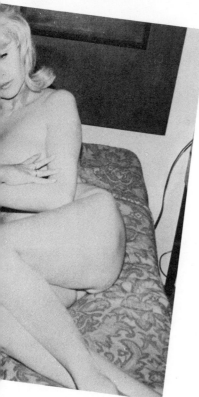

Top Randy Edwardians, remembered in *Ain't Misbehavin'* (1974), a sentimental compilation.
Above *The Snow Bunnies*, dream spinners for the raincoat market.

suddenly saw that this would provide a good opportunity of raising the whole issue.' Thus a comedy of sexual manners received more attention than it deserved, but with loud Press support that pubic hair was not in itself obscene, Trevelyan and the Censorship Board were able to lift their embargo. The following year they were involved in a wrangle over a Yugoslav movie, *The Switchboard Operator*, directed by Dusan Makavejev, which also showed pubic hair, this time on dead bodies in a mortuary. The Board was caught out by the director's lack of 'track record' and by the distributor's flippant approach to his property ('I am sending you a film which has a few tits in it. I don't think much of it but I can sell it to the sex theatres.'). Trevelyan says, 'We didn't think much of it either', but it received solid support from the critics, as has the director's later politico-satirical film *WR, Mysteries of the Organism* (1971).

For the rest of the 1960s the dark triangular patch continued to be a debating point with, for example, a flurry of discussion over Lindsay Anderson's *If* (1968) which offered a school matron in full frontal and a flash of a young girl's pubic hair in a surreal nude love scene on a café floor. An important element of this debate was the concern shown, not so much about pubic hair by itself, but about the fact that this and other revelations constituted the erotic nursery slopes from which movie-makers would soon graduate to full-blown expositions of sexual intercourse. T is has now begun to happen at various speeds in various countries. In the interim period movie-makers exercised themselves by perfecting the arts of simulated sex.

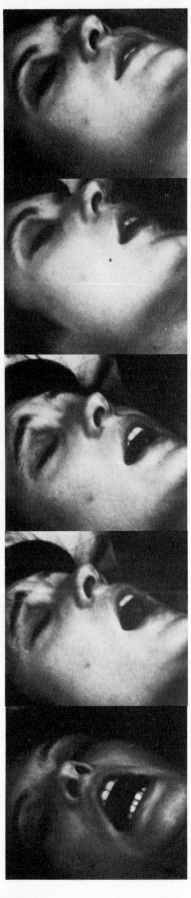

In the early '70s simulation in fact became the name of the erotic game. For many directors this meant aiming for ultra-lyrical effects, extracting a maximum of poetry from their flowing cameras, focusing on ecstatic close-ups, setting the rhythms of bodily love to evocative music, and generally seeking to dazzle by technique. There was nothing intrinsically new about this, although an illusion of innovation was occasionally achieved by an original choice of location or by an especially imaginative piece of camerawork. Thus the naked Leigh Taylor-Young seduces Ryan O'Neal on a gravestone (*The Big Bounce*, 1969); intercourse is shown reflected in the eye of a cat (*Daddy's Gone A-Hunting*); and elsewhere emphasis is given to the sheer contortions of pleasure, e.g. the 'orgasmic' face of Nicol Williamson embracing the nude Anna Karina (*Laughter in the Dark*, 1968).

But the film which broke as many totems as taboos – and earned itself a major award for brouhaha – was *I Am Curious, Yellow* (1967), directed by Vilgot Sjoman. Although the eroticism of the film was limited, its erotic appeal was considerably amplified in a written account of its contents that was prepared for Judge Paul W. LaPrade in the County Superior Court of the State of Arizona for Case No. 228092, National General Corporation versus Mummert, Sheriff of Maricopa County, heard on 8 December 1969. The report stated:

'(a) A few minutes after being introduced to Borje by her father, Lena takes him into her room where they commenced an all-night love scene. Their nude bodies were graphically depicted, head to toe, caressing while standing up, on their knees, kissing her breasts and finally lying on their backs, tired and pensive. She tells him he is number 24 but the first 19 were no fun. He lies on top of her for the obvious purpose of more intercourse. After they leave, father urinates in the wash basin. (b) Later that day Lena and Borje engage in a non-violent protest against monarchy in front of the Royal Palace in broad daylight, she takes off her panties, they straddle the balustrade, she sitting on him. The Swedish national anthem plays as they copulate in an explicit and graphic manner. (c) On retreat, Lena reads a sex manual, depicting various positions of sexual intercourse. They were clearly shown on the screen. (d) On the grass at retreat, Borje tosses Lena to the ground and he performs oral-genital acts (cunnilingus). They make love in the nude, pubic areas and genitals in full view. She caresses and kisses his penis and simulates fellatio. He caresses her genitals. (e) In the crotch of a large and ancient tree [I like that] they experiment for a good sexual intercourse position. Trousers of each are then removed and he mounts her in the tree. Intercourse is explicit and certain. (f) They struggle in a shallow pond. The scene closes with Borje nude on top of Lena, obviously having carnal knowledge. (g) Back at the ranch house, Lena and Borje again disrobe, struggle in the nude in full view. Pubic areas at close up, and he takes her from the rear as they engage in either violent sexual intercourse or sodomy. They retire to the next room on the bare floor,

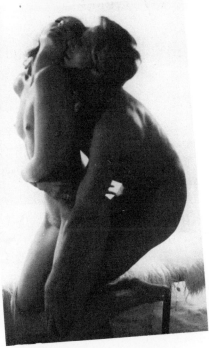

still nude, she flat on her back with loins entangled. Intercourse is clear, open and obvious. (h) The fantasy of her dream depicts her 23 lovers tied to a tree as Borje approaches. After gunning him down she solemnly takes out her knife, unbuttons his pants, pulls them down and emasculates his genitals. (i) The movie closed with Lena and Borje standing nude in full view facing camera while the hospital attendants delouse them.'

This detailed description summarizes most of the heterosexual taboos that remain either to be satirized (the film's intention) or flouted, according to one's viewpoint. Judge LaPrade found the film obscene – though in New York and New Jersey it was cleared. The case was all the more interesting (penetration and erection were *not* shown, incidentally) because, to quote the British censor (whose Board cut 11 minutes) the film was 'primarily about Swedish politics, but Sjoman had put this as a background to a sexual relationship between a young man and a girl'. The political theme was youth's revolt against political oppression and materialist values, and the film's approach to sex and nudity was stoutly defended by the director.

The other direct approach to intercourse was via sex-instruction films, a genre well-loved by German film-makers. The aims and methods of such films are usually declared to be clinical rather than erotic – even though it is self-defeating to suggest that sensuality can be separated from the processes of love-making.

In the 1960s, an ordinary enough documentary on childbirth (it showed pubic hair and a child being born) was a phenomenal box-office hit throughout Europe. This was *Helga* (1965), since when there have been numerous follow-ups, including a series from Oswalt Kolle – *The Wonder of Love*, *The Secret of Love*, *Your Wife – the Unknown Creature*, and *Your Husband – the Unknown Creature*; the latter broke the taboos on the male nude. And, in 1970, West Germany's biggest film-makers, Reginald Puhl Productions, brought out their first English-language sex-education film, *Freedom to Love*. This was directed by a Californian psychologist, Eberhard Kronhausen, and attempted a comparative survey of the world's sex laws and their effect on society. Only Sweden has gone further, showing totally explicit sexual behaviour in *The Language of Love* and *More About the Language of Love*.

When a pair of twinkling buttocks or a fiery pubic bush no longer stirred the soul, there were other taboos to tap – and many more recent films have resorted to such variants as a means of amplifying their eroticism. Press publicity, meanwhile, obligingly follows up the trends. The furore surrounding *Last Tango in Paris* (1972) is a good example: the word 'butter' acquired a new household application totally out of proportion to its significance in the film, where it acted as an aid to sodomy – though this was only one of several abuses committed on the Maria Schneider character. It is worth pointing out, too, that the loveless couplings in this film, despite being brilliantly disturbing, are essentially not what eroticism is about.

Previous pages Three scenes from the Dutch movie *Turkish Delight* (1973), nominated for an Oscar in 1974.
Left and top Moments of orgasm from the Canadian film *High*.
Centre Lena Nyman and Borje Ahlstedt in *I Am Curious, Yellow* (1967).
Above Scene from a German sex-instruction movie, *Anatomy of Love*.

RESISTANCE GROWS . . . WEAKER

Attitudes to homosexuality are one important area in which there has been a revolution in the last ten years. Where once the works of Tennessee Williams chipped slowly at reactionary strongholds, today the wishes of homosexuals and bisexuals receive wider respect – and the curiosity of non-participants, for example men wanting to see what lesbians do, has also created fresh fields for erotic movie-makers.

Far left *Pink Narcissus* featured strong-arm tactics among the boys – and an impressive line in posing pouches.
Left The old taboo of flagellation was frankly treated in Miklos Jancso's *The Round Up* (1965), where the girl is forced to run the gauntlet of the soldiers' canes.
Below Lesbian love in *Emmanuelle* (1974); Sylvia Kristel responds to the advances of Jeanne Colletin.

In America in the '50s an important source of taboo material was the work of the playwright Tennessee Williams. Because of his great insight and dramatic skill more than a hint of the tragic passions he deals with, survive in the movies – almost regardless of how much they are censored. Thus the homosexual element may have been cut out of *A Streetcar Named Desire* (1951) – Blanche's husband is simply though 'unmanly' – but not the violence and power of Brando's performance as Stanley, nor his rape of Blanche (Vivien Leigh), so essential to the plot's development. Hints of homosexuality were allowed by the time Hollywood had made *Cat on a Hot Tin Roof* (1958), and even stronger material appeared the following year in the bizarre story of *Suddenly Last Summer* (1959), which touched on the deeper taboo of cannibalism. Hollywood did not win an Oscar with an X film until *Midnight Cowboy* (1969) but by then movies had included several themes and incidents that were more than a match for the smouldering passions of Tennessee Williams's Deep South: among them was the Julie Harris character in *Reflections in a Golden Eye* (1967), written by Carson McCullers, who cuts off her nipple with a pair of garden shears.

In 1973, the British Board of Film Censors issued a record number of X certificates – 143. It is one of many statistics that can be seen as pointing the way to freedom and/or the abysmal. If the social climate has radically changed in the last fifteen years,

Some further steps on the road to greater freedom – and whatever that may bring.
Above Anne Heywood in the mirror masturbation scene in *The Fox* (1968).
Above right Anne Heywood again, braving bondage by barbed wire in *The Nun of Monza*.
Below Out of sight but very much in mind. The penis may one day make a remarkable actor, though its capabilities are for the present contained by the demands of the 'blue' market.
Right Susan George as *Twinky*, holding a torch for girls who mature early.

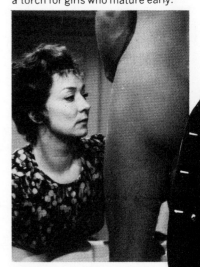

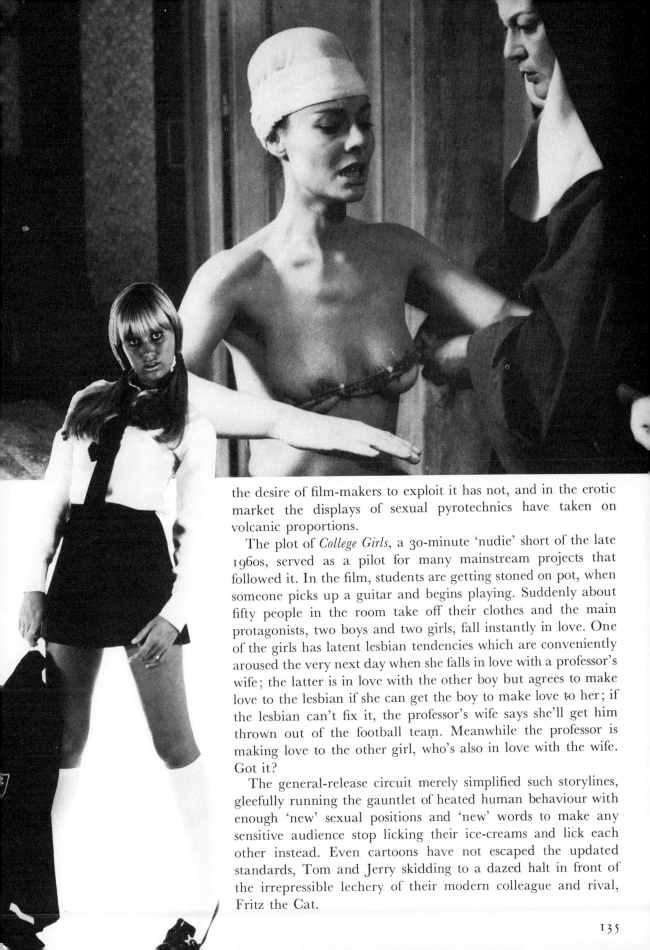

the desire of film-makers to exploit it has not, and in the erotic market the displays of sexual pyrotechnics have taken on volcanic proportions.

The plot of *College Girls*, a 30-minute 'nudie' short of the late 1960s, served as a pilot for many mainstream projects that followed it. In the film, students are getting stoned on pot, when someone picks up a guitar and begins playing. Suddenly about fifty people in the room take off their clothes and the main protagonists, two boys and two girls, fall instantly in love. One of the girls has latent lesbian tendencies which are conveniently aroused the very next day when she falls in love with a professor's wife; the latter is in love with the other boy but agrees to make love to the lesbian if she can get the boy to make love to her; if the lesbian can't fix it, the professor's wife says she'll get him thrown out of the football team. Meanwhile the professor is making love to the other girl, who's also in love with the wife. Got it?

The general-release circuit merely simplified such storylines, gleefully running the gauntlet of heated human behaviour with enough 'new' sexual positions and 'new' words to make any sensitive audience stop licking their ice-creams and lick each other instead. Even cartoons have not escaped the updated standards, Tom and Jerry skidding to a dazed halt in front of the irrepressible lechery of their modern colleague and rival, Fritz the Cat.

Problems of Violence

A more difficult area for erotic assessment is the present dominating issue of movie violence, which obviously has strong sexual connections – in its oldest form, raping and flogging, in its newest, buggery and bondage. A long catalogue of violence would seem a bit 'heavy' in this text, so two titles and a single country's attitude must suffice. *The Story of O*, which to some is Europe's most famous modern pornographic novel, concerns the purification of a fashion photographer who submits herself to every form of physical abuse in the name of love for her fiancé. The abusers are his friends, the location an exclusive country chateâu. There has been more than one attempt to film it, none successful as movies on the level of the original work. On a simpler, mass-market basis, the theme is regularly explored; an old favourite in membership movie houses, for example, was predictably called *Whips and Women* (1964).

But it is the Japanese who have specialized above all others in the eroticism to be gained from bullying the flesh. Donald Richie in an interesting article about Japanese eroductions (a portmanteau term they coined from 'erotic productions') explained something of the background. Up to 1973 at least, pubic hair was being fiercely (and literally) attacked in Japan. Thus in the American pop festival film, *Woodstock*, nude background couples had emulsion scraped from the offending parts so that they 'seemed girded with fireworks'. It is important also to bear in mind that Japan has a fixed ban on hard-core pornography. That said, the humiliations of the flesh that are featured in the typical eroduction, must seem bizarrely near the borderline to Western eyes. As Donald Richie describes them, they feature bar hostesses and good-time girls in scenes where 'in order to escape, women must run nude through the streets; scenes where nude or near nude women are overtaken in muddy rice-paddies, knocked down, mauled, and dirtied by their attackers; scenes where women are blackmailed into, or in other ways compelled to give themselves to, various perversions, the overwhelmingly most common being tied up, hung by the wrists, being savagely beaten, being otherwise mistreated with sticks, lighted candles, and – oddly, but an eroduction favourite – long-handled shoe-horns.'

By international standards – if such a vast generalization can be made – the erotic appeal of such scenes would seem limited to a small sector of the market. Japan, however, is a land long accustomed to ritualized violence, and erotic standards can be expected to differ. Some clue to these differences may lie in Japan's massive overcrowding. As a nation, sardine-packed into their legendary commuter trains, the Japanese have become a forcing house whose aim is perfect miniaturism, whether in terms of transistor radios or flower gardens. Such compression carries obvious dangers, even for people accustomed to it, and so the Japanese have devised a number of safety valves. To the martial arts can now be added the eroduction.

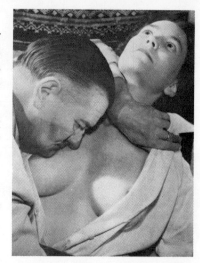

Above the chilling needs of the necrophile are seen to be satisfied in this scene from the French movie, *Les Impures*.

Above Sex by force in *Drive, He Said* (1971), directed by Jack Nicholson and featuring Mike Margotta and Karen Black.
Above right Rape in the Old West; from *The Scavengers*.
Right Fritz the Cat . . . perkier than Micky Mouse, but then girl cats didn't have the breasts on them that they evidently do today.

Above The brutal moods of the Japanese receive plenty of outlets at the movies, where such films are known as eroductions, a contraction of 'erotic productions'.

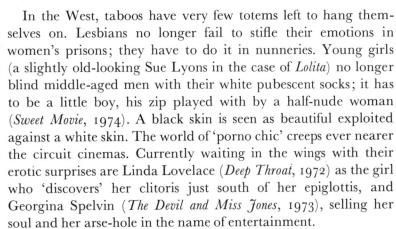

In the West, taboos have very few totems left to hang themselves on. Lesbians no longer fail to stifle their emotions in women's prisons; they have to do it in nunneries. Young girls (a slightly old-looking Sue Lyons in the case of *Lolita*) no longer blind middle-aged men with their white pubescent socks; it has to be a little boy, his zip played with by a half-nude woman (*Sweet Movie*, 1974). A black skin is seen as beautiful exploited against a white skin. The world of 'porno chic' creeps ever nearer the circuit cinemas. Currently waiting in the wings with their erotic surprises are Linda Lovelace (*Deep Throat*, 1972) as the girl who 'discovers' her clitoris just south of her epiglottis, and Georgina Spelvin (*The Devil and Miss Jones*, 1973), selling her soul and her arse-hole in the name of entertainment.

It all seems a long way away from the day when Shelley Winters made her famous remark about nudity on the stage. She said: 'I think it is disgusting, shameful and damaging to all things American. But if I were 22 with a great body, it would be artistic, tasteful, patriotic and a progressive religious experience.'

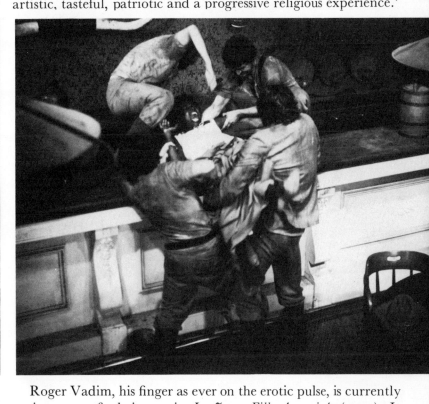

Roger Vadim, his finger as ever on the erotic pulse, is currently trying out a fresh image in *La Jeune Fille Assassinée* (1975). It includes a scene where a man makes love to a girl who has been killed. Twenty years before, he had discovered Brigitte Bardot. Fifteen years ago, in Clouzot's *La Vérité*, she had swung her slim, sensual body out of bed; her bare legs are seen in close-up as she dances a rhumba across to the window. Cut to her dishevelled hair and a wriggle of her naked bottom. Dancing was a key to her brilliant eroticism, and no one needed beaver shots to help her achieve it.

Overleaf And now, when she's ready, the lady on the front cover will see you out.

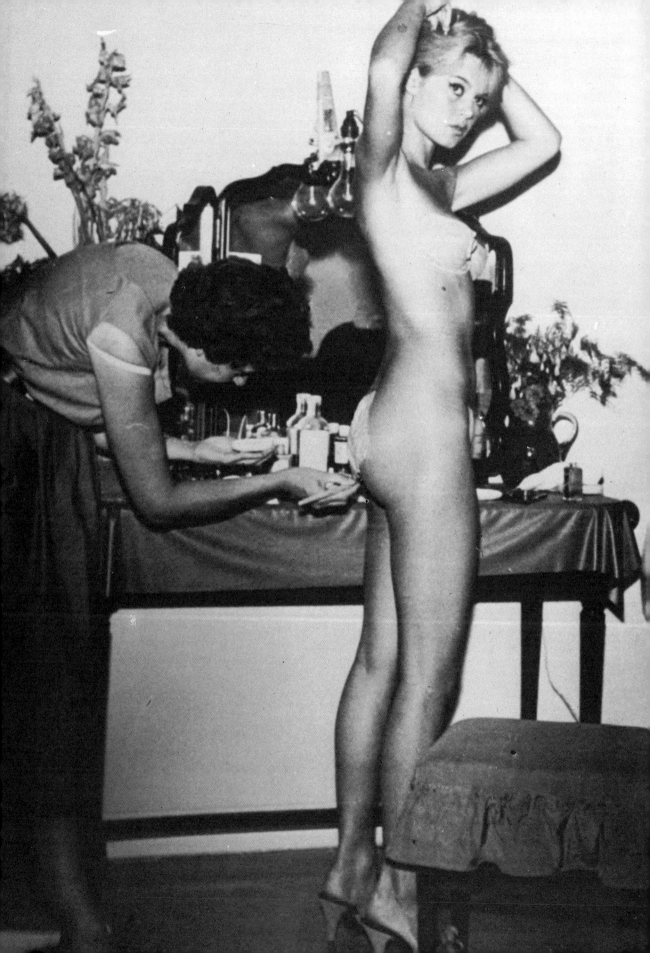

ACKNOWLEDGEMENTS
The author and Roxby Press Ltd wish to thank the authors of the following source books: Brownlow, Kevin *The Parade's Gone By*; Cary, John *The Story of Epic Films*; Halliwell, Leslie *Picturegoers Companion*; Hanson, Gilliam *Original Skin*; Knight, Arthur and Alpert, Hollis Playboy's *History of Sex in the Cinema*; Robinson, David *World Cinema*; Schein, Harry *Shots in the Dark*; Schumach, Harry *The Face on the Cutting Room Floor*; Tyler, Parker *75 Classics of the Foreign Film* and *Sex, Psyche, Etcetera in the Film*; Walker, Alexander *Stardom* and *Sex in the Movies* and Wood, Robin.

Roxby Press Ltd extends special thanks for their help in providing illustrations to the Gideon Bachmann Collection, Tony Crawley, and the British Film Institute Stills Department. Other Illustrations were kindly supplied by Avco Embassy Pictures (UK) Ltd., British Lion Film Distributors Ltd., The Cinema Bookshop, Davidson and Dalling, The Kobal Collection, Rex Features Ltd., S F Distributors Ltd., and United Artists Corporation Ltd.

Roxby Press Ltd also gratefully acknowledges the co-operation of Anglo-EMI Film Distributors Ltd, C.I.C. Film Distributors Ltd, Columbia Warner Film Distributors Ltd, Fox Rank Film Distributors Ltd., Hemdale Film Distributors Ltd.

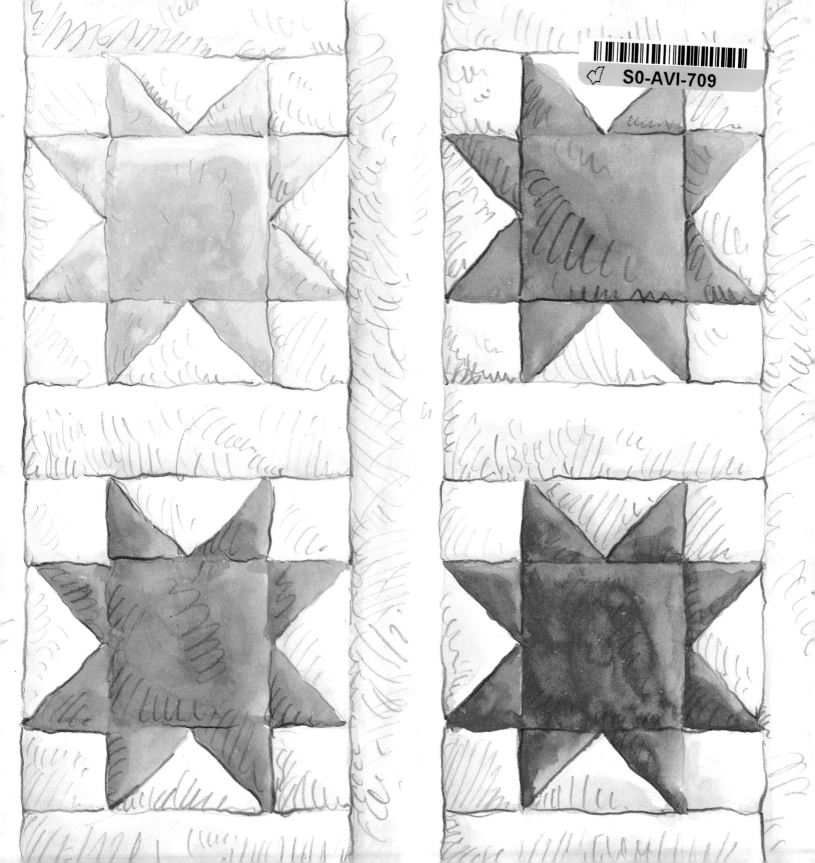

Before I Was Born

By Harriet Ziefert
Illustrated by Rufus Coes

Alfred A. Knopf
New York

This is a Borzoi Book published by Alfred A. Knopf, Inc.

Text copyright © 1989 by Harriet Ziefert. Illustrations copyright © 1989 by Rufus Coes. All rights reserved under International and Pan-American Copyright Conventions. Published in the United States by Alfred A. Knopf, Inc., New York, and simultaneously in Canada by Random House of Canada Limited, Toronto. Distributed by Random House, Inc., New York.

Library of Congress Cataloging-in-Publication Data

Ziefert, Harriet.
    Before I was born.
    Summary: A child relates how Papa built a cradle and Mama made a quilt in preparation for the birth of their baby.
    ISBN 0-394-85128-5
    ISBN 0-394-95128-X (lib. bdg.)
    [1. Parent and child—Fiction. 2. Babies—Fiction] I. Coes, Rufus, ill. II. Title. PZ7.Z487Bh 1989 [E] 88-37255

Manufactured in Singapore for Harriet Ziefert, Inc.

1 2 3 4 5 6 7 8 9 0

For Jon and Jamie & for Jon and Ben
H. M. Z.

For Emily, Julia, Michelle, Nellie, Ben and Put
R. C.

A long time ago, before I was born, Papa made a cradle and Mama made a quilt.

Papa bought clear white pine.

Mama found bright-colored cloth.

Papa sawed the wood.

Mama cut the cloth.

Papa glued and hammered…

until the cradle could stand alone
on its wooden rockers.

Mama snipped and sewed…

until the quilt was just the right size.

Papa painted the cradle to make it smooth and pretty.

Mama stuffed the quilt with cotton
to make it warm and fluffy.

A long time ago, before I was born, Papa and Mama made sure everything was ready.

And when I was just a new baby,
Papa rocked the cradle gently
while Mama sang a lullaby.